The Manif
Blueprint

Cracking the Code
to Abundance

By Christopher Galantier

Published by Healthy Lifestyles for All

Table of Contents

Introduction

Welcome to "The Manifestation Blueprint: Cracking the Code to Abundance." Are you ready to unlock the secrets to manifesting your dreams and creating a life filled with abundance? In this transformative journey, we will dive deep into the principles and practices that will empower you to tap into your inner potential and manifest your deepest desires. Let's have a look at what's included in this book.

Chapter 1: The Power of Manifestation: Unleashing Your Inner Potential
Discover the extraordinary power within you and learn how to harness it to manifest the life you've always envisioned. Explore the unlimited possibilities that await you when you tap into your inherent ability to create your reality.

Chapter 2: Understanding the Law of Attraction: Creating Your Reality
Unravel the mysteries of the Law of Attraction and learn how your thoughts and emotions shape the world around you. Gain a profound understanding of the universal principles that govern manifestation and learn to use them to your advantage.

Chapter 3: The Art of Visualization: Painting Your Dreams into Existence
Learn the transformative practice of visualization and how it can help you vividly imagine and attract the life you desire. Discover the techniques to create detailed mental images that inspire and align your actions with your aspirations.

Chapter 4: Harnessing the Energy of Manifestation: Aligning Your Thoughts and Emotions
Explore the essential connection between your thoughts and emotions and how they influence the manifestation process. Master techniques to align your inner world with your desired outcomes and amplify your manifesting power.

Chapter 5: Setting Clear Intentions: Navigating Your Path to Success
Discover the importance of setting clear and powerful intentions as the guiding compass on your journey to manifestation. Learn practical strategies to define your goals, infuse them with purpose, and stay focused on your desired outcomes.

Chapter 6: Overcoming Limiting Beliefs: Rewriting Your Subconscious Mind
Uncover and release the limiting beliefs that have held you back from manifesting abundance. Discover effective techniques to reprogram your subconscious mind and replace self-sabotaging patterns with empowering beliefs that support your manifestation journey.

Chapter 7: Cultivating Gratitude and Abundance: Opening the Floodgates of Manifestation
Learn the transformative practice of gratitude and how it can shift your perspective, attract more abundance, and amplify your manifestation power. Discover powerful gratitude rituals and exercises to cultivate a mindset of abundance.

Chapter 8: Creating Wealth and Prosperity: Abundance as Your Birthright
Delve into the realm of wealth and prosperity and embrace the belief that abundance is your birthright. Explore strategies to attract financial abundance, create multiple streams of income, and manifest a life of prosperity in all areas.

Chapter 9: Manifesting Health and Well-being: Nurturing Your Body, Mind, and Spirit
Uncover the secrets to manifesting optimal health and well-being. Discover the interconnectedness of your body, mind, and spirit and learn practices that support holistic well-being, including self-care, mindfulness, and nurturing lifestyle choices.

Chapter 10: Role of Patience and Trust: Surrendering to the Timing of the Universe

Recognize the vital role of patience and trust in the manifestation process. Learn how to surrender to the divine timing of the universe, overcome impatience and doubt, and cultivate the unwavering belief that your desires are on their way.

Get ready to embark on an enlightening and transformative journey as we crack the code to abundance. The Manifestation Blueprint will provide you with the tools, insights, and practices you need to manifest your dreams and create a life of unlimited possibilities. It's time to embrace your power and step into a reality where abundance is your natural state. Let's begin this remarkable adventure together!

Chapter 1: The Power of Manifestation: Unleashing Your Inner Potential

Welcome to "The Power of Manifestation: Unleashing Your Inner Potential," a journey of self-discovery and transformation. In this book, we will delve into the fascinating realm of manifestation and explore the depths of your inner potential. So, grab a hot beverage, find a cozy spot, and let's embark on this empowering exploration together.

Manifestation is the process of bringing your desires, dreams, and aspirations into physical reality. It is the art of consciously creating your own destiny. When you manifest, you tap into the universal energy and collaborate with it to shape your life according to your intentions.

Think of manifestation as a powerful magnet that attracts the experiences, people, and circumstances that align with your thoughts, beliefs, and emotions. It is a co-creative process where you become an active participant in shaping your reality.

Within each of us lies a wellspring of untapped potential, waiting to be unleashed. Your inner potential encompasses your unique talents, strengths, passions, and purpose. It is the essence of who you are and the limitless possibilities that reside within you.

Unleashing your inner potential means recognizing and nurturing your authentic self. It involves harnessing your inherent abilities and channeling them towards achieving your goals and creating a fulfilling life. When you tap into your inner potential, you unlock a reservoir of creativity, resilience, and personal power that can propel you towards extraordinary achievements.

This book will serve as your guide to discover and unlock the dormant potential within you. Through practical exercises, insights, and tools, we will explore various techniques that can assist you in manifesting your desires and awakening your inner potential.

So, if you're ready to embark on a transformative journey of self-discovery and empowerment, let's dive deep into the profound world of manifestation. Get ready to unlock the doors to a life of purpose, abundance, and joy as we unveil the power that resides within you.

Part 1: Understanding the Law of Attraction

To unleash the *Power of Manifestation*, it is crucial to understand the fundamental principle that governs it—the Law of Attraction. This universal law operates at the core of our existence, shaping our reality based on the thoughts and emotions we emit into the world. In this section, we will explore the essence of the Law of Attraction, how our thoughts and emotions influence our experiences, and the profound connection between our inner world and external outcomes.

A. Explaining the Law of Attraction

The Law of Attraction is a principle that states that like attracts like. In simpler terms, it means that the energy we emit into the universe, through our thoughts, emotions, and beliefs, magnetically draws similar energies or experiences back to us. This law recognizes that everything in the universe is made up of energy, and our thoughts and emotions carry their own unique vibrational frequencies.

Imagine your thoughts and emotions as energetic beacons that send out signals to the universe, signaling your desires and expectations. The Law of Attraction responds to these signals by bringing into your life people, situations, and circumstances that align with the vibrational frequency you are emitting. In other words, your predominant thoughts and emotions become the blueprint for what you attract and experience.

B. How Thoughts and Emotions Shape Reality

Our thoughts and emotions are not mere fleeting occurrences. They possess immense creative power and serve as the building blocks of our reality. Thoughts are like seeds planted in the fertile soil of the universe, while emotions are the nourishing waters that help those seeds grow.

When you consistently focus on positive, empowering thoughts and cultivate emotions such as joy, gratitude, and love, you align yourself with higher vibrations. This alignment sets into motion a chain of events that attract corresponding positive experiences and outcomes into your life. Conversely, if you dwell on negative thoughts, fears, and limitations, you inadvertently invite similar energies and experiences into your reality.

C. Recognizing the Connection Between Thoughts and Outcomes

The Law of Attraction reminds us of the power of our thoughts and emotions in shaping our lives. It is not merely wishful thinking or idle daydreaming; it is a profound understanding of the interplay between our inner world and the external reality we experience.

By recognizing the connection between our thoughts and outcomes, we become conscious creators of our lives. We take responsibility for the energy we project and the experiences we attract. This awareness empowers us to choose our thoughts wisely and cultivate positive emotions that support our desires and goals.

Summary

Understanding the Law of Attraction opens the gateway to deliberate manifestation. It teaches us that our thoughts and emotions are potent forces that influence our reality. By aligning our thoughts and emotions with our desired outcomes, we can proactively attract and create the life we envision. In the following chapters, we will explore practical techniques and strategies to harness the power of the Law of Attraction and leverage it in our manifestation journey. So, get ready to unlock the secrets of manifestation and embark on a transformative path towards a life of abundance, joy, and fulfilment.

Part 2: Aligning with Your Desires

Manifestation is not a random process; it requires conscious alignment with your desires and goals. In this section, we will delve into the importance of aligning with your desires, exploring techniques to identify your true aspirations, clarifying your intentions and priorities, and cultivating a positive mindset that supports your manifestation journey. Get ready to connect with your deepest desires and set the stage for their manifestation.

A. Identifying Your True Desires and Goals

Before you can align with your desires, it is essential to uncover what truly resonates with your heart and soul. Take a moment to reflect and explore your passions, dreams, and aspirations. Ask yourself, "What brings me joy? What do I long to create or experience in my life?"

Listen to the whispers of your intuition and trust the innate wisdom within you. Your true desires may evolve over time, but at this moment, they serve as a compass guiding you towards a life of fulfilment. As you identify your authentic desires, you pave the way for their manifestation.

B. Clarifying Your Intentions and Priorities

Once you have identified your true desires, it is crucial to clarify your intentions and priorities. Intentions act as the guiding lights that illuminate your path and keep you focused. Take the time to define your intentions with clarity and specificity. What do you intend to manifest? How do you want to feel? What steps are you willing to take to bring your desires to fruition?

Additionally, prioritize your desires to ensure that you allocate your time, energy, and resources effectively. Prioritization helps you avoid overwhelm and enables you to dedicate your attention to what truly matters. By aligning your intentions and setting clear priorities, you create a roadmap towards the realization of your dreams.

C. Cultivating a Positive Mindset

A positive mindset is a catalyst for manifestation. It empowers you to overcome challenges, navigate setbacks, and maintain unwavering belief in the possibilities that lie ahead. Cultivating a positive mindset involves consciously choosing thoughts that support your desires and reframing any negative self-talk or limiting beliefs.

Practice self-awareness and observe the quality of your thoughts. Are they empowering, uplifting, and aligned with your desires? If not, gently redirect them towards more positive and supportive narratives. Surround yourself with positive influences, engage in activities that uplift your spirit, and embrace a mindset of gratitude and possibility.

Summary
Aligning with your desires is a transformative step towards manifestation. By identifying your true desires, clarifying your intentions and priorities, and cultivating a positive mindset, you establish a strong foundation for the manifestation process. As you embark on this journey, remember that alignment is not a one-time task; it is an ongoing practice. Regularly reassess your desires, intentions, and mindset to ensure they remain aligned with your evolving self. In the upcoming chapters, we will explore additional techniques and practices that will further enhance your alignment and propel you towards the manifestation of your dreams. So, stay committed, stay aligned, and get ready to witness the magic unfold in your life.

Part 3: Visualization Techniques

Visualization is a powerful tool in the manifestation process, allowing you to paint vivid mental images of your goals and desired outcomes. In this section, we will explore the role of visualization in manifestation, the process of visualizing goals and desired outcomes, and how incorporating sensory details can enhance the effectiveness of your visualization practice. Get ready to tap into the creative power of your mind and bring your dreams to life through visualization.

A. The Role of Visualization in Manifestation

Visualization is the process of creating clear and detailed mental images of what you desire to manifest. It serves as a bridge between your imagination and the physical reality you wish to create. Visualization harnesses the power of your mind to shape your thoughts and emotions, aligning them with your desired outcomes and sending a powerful signal to the universe.

By vividly visualizing your goals and desires, you strengthen your belief in their realization. Visualization activates the Reticular Activating System (RAS) in your brain, which heightens your awareness of opportunities and resources that can support your manifestation journey. It also cultivates a positive mindset, enhances focus, and nurtures a deep sense of alignment with your aspirations.

B. Visualizing Goals and Desired Outcomes

To harness the full potential of visualization, begin by clearly defining your goals and desired outcomes. Take time to articulate what you want to manifest and imagine it as if it has already been achieved. Create a mental movie or a series of images that represent your desired reality.

Engage your senses as you visualize. See the vibrant colors, hear the sounds, and feel the textures associated with your desired outcome. Immerse yourself in the experience as if you are living it in the present moment. Allow yourself to feel the joy, gratitude, and fulfilment that come with manifesting your desires.

Consistency is key when it comes to visualization. Set aside dedicated time each day to practice visualization, preferably in a quiet and relaxed environment. The more you engage with your visualization practice, the more potent and effective it becomes.

C. Incorporating Sensory Details for Enhanced Visualization

To supercharge your visualization practice, incorporate sensory details into your mental images. Engaging multiple senses helps to create a richer and more immersive experience, amplifying the emotional charge and realism of your visualizations.

For instance, if your desire is to travel to a tropical beach, visualize the vibrant blue hues of the ocean, feel the warmth of the sun on your skin, taste the saltiness of the sea breeze, and listen to the rhythmic sounds of the waves crashing against the shore. By incorporating sensory details, you tap into the power of your imagination and create a more vivid and compelling visualization.

Summary
Visualization is a potent technique that harnesses the creative power of your mind to manifest your desires. By visualizing your goals and desired outcomes with clarity and emotion, you activate the Law of Attraction and align yourself with the abundant possibilities of the universe. Remember to consistently practice visualization, engaging your senses and immersing yourself in the experience. In the following chapters, we will explore additional manifestation techniques that complement and enhance the power of visualization. So, keep visualizing, keep believing, and watch as your dreams unfold before your eyes.

Part 4: Affirmations and Mantras

Affirmations and mantras are potent tools that can reprogram your mind, aligning your thoughts and beliefs with your desired reality. In this section, we will explore the power of positive affirmations, the art of crafting effective affirmations for manifestation, and the importance of daily practice and repetition to reinforce their impact. Get ready to embrace the transformative potential of affirmations and mantras on your manifestation journey.

A. Harnessing the Power of Positive Affirmations

Affirmations are positive statements that you repeat to yourself to shift your mindset and beliefs. They serve as powerful reminders of your inherent worth, capabilities, and potential. Affirmations work by rewiring your neural pathways, replacing negative or limiting thoughts with empowering and supportive ones.

When you consistently reinforce positive affirmations, you activate the Law of Attraction and align your energy with the experiences and outcomes you desire. Affirmations have the ability to reprogram your subconscious mind, influencing your thoughts, emotions, and actions in alignment with your aspirations.

B. Crafting Effective Affirmations for Manifestation

Crafting effective affirmations involves creating statements that resonate with your desires and beliefs. Here are some guidelines to help you create powerful affirmations:

1. Use the present tense: Phrase your affirmations as if your desired outcome has already manifested. For example, instead of saying, "I will be successful," state, "I am successful."
2. Be positive and empowering: Frame your affirmations in a positive and empowering manner. Focus on what you want to attract and experience, rather than what you want to avoid or eliminate.
3. Make them specific and specific: Be specific about what you want to manifest. This helps to sharpen your focus and enhances the effectiveness of your affirmations. For example, instead of saying, "I am financially abundant," you can say, "I am attracting wealth and abundance in all areas of my life."
4. Use emotion and belief: Infuse your affirmations with emotion and belief. Feel the truth and power of your affirmations as you repeat them, allowing them to evoke a sense of excitement, joy, and gratitude within you.

C. Daily Practice and Repetition for Reinforcement

Consistency is key when it comes to affirmations. Make it a daily practice to repeat your affirmations, preferably in the morning when your mind is receptive and open. Find a quiet space, take a few deep breaths, and repeat your affirmations with conviction and belief.

Repetition plays a vital role in reinforcing the impact of affirmations. The more you repeat your affirmations, the more they sink into your subconscious mind, replacing old patterns and beliefs. Consider using visual aids such as sticky notes or affirmation cards to remind yourself of your affirmations throughout the day.

Integrate your affirmations into your daily routine and rituals. Repeat them while you meditate, during your morning routine, or before you sleep. Embrace them as a part of your mindset and let them guide your thoughts, actions, and decisions.

Summary

Affirmations and mantras are transformative tools that enable you to reprogram your mind and align your thoughts and beliefs with your desired reality. By harnessing the power of positive affirmations, crafting effective statements, and practicing daily repetition, you empower yourself to manifest your desires and create a life of abundance and fulfilment. In the upcoming chapters, we will explore additional techniques and strategies that complement the power of affirmations. So, keep affirming, keep believing, and watch as your affirmations pave the way for your dreams to come true.

Part 5: Overcoming Limiting Beliefs

Limiting beliefs can act as roadblocks on your manifestation journey, hindering your progress and holding you back from reaching your full potential. In this section, we will explore the process of identifying and challenging limiting beliefs, rewriting negative thought patterns, and cultivating self-belief and confidence. Get ready to break free from the constraints of your mind and step into a realm of limitless possibilities.

A. Identifying and Challenging Limiting Beliefs

Limiting beliefs are deeply ingrained thoughts and beliefs that create self-imposed limitations on what you believe is possible for yourself. To overcome them, start by becoming aware of their presence. Pay attention to recurring negative thoughts or self-defeating patterns that arise in your mind.

Once you identify a limiting belief, challenge its validity. Ask yourself, "Is this belief based on facts or assumptions? How has this belief been holding me back? Is there evidence to the contrary?" Recognize that limiting beliefs are often irrational and unfounded, stemming from past experiences or societal conditioning.

Confront your limiting beliefs with empowering questions and counterarguments. Reframe them into positive and supportive beliefs that align with your desires and aspirations. Replace self-doubt with self-belief and embrace the notion that you are capable of achieving greatness.

B. Rewriting Negative Thought Patterns

Negative thought patterns can reinforce limiting beliefs and sabotage your manifestation efforts. To overcome them, it is essential to rewire your mind with positive and empowering thoughts. Begin by observing your thought patterns and noticing when negative thoughts arise.

When a negative thought surfaces, consciously challenge it and replace it with a positive affirmation or a more empowering perspective. For example, if you catch yourself thinking, "I'm not good enough," reframe it as, "I am worthy and capable of achieving my goals."

Consistency is key when it comes to rewiring negative thought patterns. Practice self-awareness and be vigilant about your thoughts. Whenever a negative thought arises, consciously redirect it towards a positive and supportive belief. Over time, this process will help you reprogram your mind and establish new, empowering thought patterns.

C. Cultivating Self-Belief and Confidence

To overcome limiting beliefs, it is crucial to cultivate self-belief and confidence. Start by celebrating your strengths, talents, and past accomplishments. Reflect on your abilities and acknowledge the obstacles you have already overcome. Embrace a growth mindset and see challenges as opportunities for growth and learning.

Surround yourself with positive influences and supportive individuals who uplift and encourage you. Seek out mentors or role models who have achieved what you aspire to accomplish. Their success stories can inspire and reinforce your belief in what is possible for you.

Engage in daily practices that nurture self-belief and confidence, such as affirmations, visualization, and self-care. Embrace self-compassion and practice positive self-talk. Treat yourself with kindness and celebrate even the smallest victories along your journey.

Summary

Overcoming limiting beliefs is a transformative step towards manifesting your desires and unlocking your true potential. By identifying and challenging limiting beliefs, rewriting negative thought patterns, and cultivating self-belief and confidence, you break free from the shackles of self-doubt and open yourself to a world of limitless possibilities.

Remember, this process requires self-awareness, consistency, and a commitment to personal growth. It may take time and effort, but the rewards are immeasurable. As you embark on this journey of overcoming limiting beliefs, stay patient, stay determined, and watch as your newfound belief in yourself propels you towards the manifestation of your dreams.

Part 6: Taking Inspired Action

Manifestation is not solely reliant on positive thoughts and beliefs; it also requires taking inspired action. In this section, we will explore the importance of action in manifestation, the significance of aligning actions with intentions and goals, and the transformative power of embracing opportunities and stepping out of comfort zones. Get ready to activate your dreams through purposeful and inspired action.

A. The Importance of Action in Manifestation

While thoughts and beliefs lay the foundation for manifestation, it is through action that you bring your desires into tangible reality. Action is the catalyst that bridges the gap between where you are and where you want to be. It demonstrates your commitment, dedication, and willingness to actively participate in the manifestation process.

Action sends a powerful message to the universe that you are ready to receive and co-create with the abundant possibilities that surround you. It propels you forward, opens doors of opportunity, and attracts synchronicities that align with your intentions. Remember, the universe rewards those who take aligned and inspired action.

B. Aligning Actions with Intentions and Goals

To manifest your desires effectively, it is essential to align your actions with your intentions and goals. Begin by clarifying your intentions and defining specific action steps that will move you closer to your desired outcomes. Break down your goals into smaller, actionable tasks that are achievable and realistic.

Ensure that your actions are in alignment with your values and beliefs. Consider whether the actions you are taking support the manifestation of your desires or if they are incongruent with your true aspirations. By consciously aligning your actions with your intentions, you create a powerful synergy that propels you forward on your manifestation journey.

C. Embracing Opportunities and Stepping Out of Comfort Zones

To manifest your desires, it is crucial to embrace opportunities and step out of your comfort zones. The path to manifestation often requires venturing into the unknown and taking risks. Recognize that growth and expansion happen beyond the boundaries of familiarity.

Be open to recognizing and seizing opportunities that come your way. Sometimes, they may not align with your preconceived plans but could lead to unexpected blessings. Trust your intuition and embrace the flow of synchronicities that guide you towards your desires.

Stepping out of your comfort zone is an act of courage and faith. It involves facing fears and overcoming self-imposed limitations. Embrace discomfort as a sign of growth and view challenges as opportunities for learning and expansion. By pushing past your comfort zone, you create space for new possibilities and elevate your manifestation potential.

Summary

Taking inspired action is a vital component of the manifestation process. By aligning your actions with your intentions and goals, you demonstrate your commitment to manifesting your desires. Embrace opportunities and step out of your comfort zones, knowing that growth and transformation happen beyond familiarity. As you take purposeful and inspired action, watch how the universe responds, bringing you closer to the manifestation of your dreams. So, stay proactive, stay open, and watch as your actions become the bridge that connects your dreams to your reality.

Part 7: Gratitude and Manifestation

Gratitude is a powerful manifestation tool that can transform your perspective and attract abundance into your life. In this section, we will explore the role of gratitude in manifestation, the importance of appreciating the present moment and blessings, and how a grateful mindset can magnetize abundance into your reality. Get ready to unlock the transformative power of gratitude and infuse your manifestation journey with a sense of appreciation and abundance.

A. Cultivating Gratitude as a Manifestation Tool

Gratitude is a state of being that acknowledges and appreciates the blessings and abundance in your life. It is a powerful tool that shifts your focus from what is lacking to what you already have. By cultivating gratitude, you elevate your vibrational frequency and align yourself with the positive energies of manifestation.

To cultivate gratitude, make it a daily practice to express gratitude for the simple things in life. Take a few moments each day to reflect on and appreciate the blessings, opportunities, and experiences that you are grateful for. Keep a gratitude journal where you can jot down the things you appreciate and reflect on them regularly.

B. Appreciating the Present Moment and Blessings

Gratitude invites you to embrace the present moment fully and appreciate the abundance that surrounds you. Often, we get caught up in striving for future goals and desires, overlooking the blessings and opportunities that exist in the present.

Take time each day to be fully present and mindful of the present moment. Notice the beauty in nature, savor the taste of your meals, and appreciate the warmth of a smile from a loved one. By immersing yourself in the present moment and cultivating gratitude for the little things, you create a foundation of positivity and attract more blessings into your life.

C. Attracting Abundance through a Grateful Mindset

A grateful mindset is a magnet for abundance. When you approach life with gratitude, you open yourself to receive more blessings, opportunities, and abundance. The Law of

Attraction responds to your vibrational frequency, and gratitude elevates your vibration to align with the frequency of abundance.

Embrace a grateful mindset by consciously shifting your focus from scarcity to abundance. Instead of dwelling on what you lack, focus on the abundance that already exists in your life. Practice affirmations of gratitude, expressing appreciation for the wealth, love, health, and opportunities that come your way.

As you cultivate a grateful mindset, you begin to notice synchronicities and opportunities that align with your desires. The universe responds to your gratitude by bringing forth more experiences and manifestations that evoke feelings of gratitude. Embrace the cycle of gratitude and abundance, and watch as your manifestations unfold with grace and ease.

Summary

Gratitude is a transformative tool that can elevate your manifestation journey to new heights. By cultivating gratitude as a manifestation tool, appreciating the present moment and blessings, and attracting abundance through a grateful mindset, you open the floodgates of abundance in your life. Embrace gratitude as a way of being, and watch as your reality becomes infused with blessings, opportunities, and manifestations that reflect your deepest desires. So, express gratitude, appreciate the present, and allow the magic of gratitude to enhance your manifestation journey.

Part 8: Patience and Trust in the Process

Patience and trust are essential qualities to cultivate on your manifestation journey. In this section, we will explore the importance of embracing the unfolding of manifestation, letting go of attachment, and surrendering to the universe. We will also delve into the significance of trusting in divine timing and guidance. By embodying patience and trust, you can navigate the manifestation process with grace and allow your desires to manifest in perfect timing. So, let's dive in and discover the power of patience and trust in the process.

A. Embracing the Unfolding of Manifestation
Manifestation is not always an instant process. It requires patience and the ability to embrace the natural unfolding of events. Often, there is a divine orchestration at play, aligning the necessary elements and experiences to bring your desires to fruition.

Embrace the unfolding of manifestation by releasing the need for immediate results. Trust that everything is happening in divine order and that each step forward, no matter how small, is taking you closer to your desired outcome. Recognize that the journey itself holds valuable lessons and growth opportunities.

B. Letting Go of Attachment and Surrendering to the Universe
Attachment can hinder the manifestation process. When you cling too tightly to a specific outcome or become fixated on how and when your desires should manifest, you create resistance. This resistance blocks the natural flow of abundance and limits the possibilities that the universe can bring forth.

Practice letting go of attachment by surrendering to the universe. Release your grip on the specifics and instead focus on the essence and feeling of what you desire. Trust that the universe knows the best way to bring your desires into reality and relinquish control over the how and when.

Surrendering to the universe does not mean giving up or being passive; rather, it is an act of trust and surrendering to the greater wisdom at work. It is about aligning your energy with your desires and allowing the universe to work its magic in its own time and way.

C. Trusting in Divine Timing and Guidance
Divine timing plays a significant role in manifestation. Trust that everything happens at the right time and in the right order. Sometimes, the universe orchestrates events and synchronicities behind the scenes to align all the necessary elements for your desires to manifest in the most perfect and aligned way.

Cultivate trust in divine timing by recognizing that the universe has a bigger perspective and knows what is best for you. Trust that delays or detours are not obstacles but rather opportunities for growth, preparation, or redirection. Have faith that the universe is guiding you towards your desires, even when the path seems uncertain.

In addition to trusting in divine timing, trust in the guidance you receive along the way. Pay attention to your intuition, signs, and synchronicities that offer guidance and support. Trust that the universe is always providing you with the necessary tools, insights, and opportunities to manifest your desires.

Summary
Patience and trust are vital qualities to cultivate on your manifestation journey. Embrace the unfolding of manifestation, letting go of attachment, and surrendering to the universe. Trust in divine timing and guidance, knowing that everything is happening in perfect order. As you embody patience and trust, you align your energy with the natural flow of abundance and allow your desires to manifest with ease and grace. So, practice patience, surrender to the process, and trust in the wisdom of the universe as you manifest your dreams into reality.

Part 9: Manifestation and Self-Reflection
Self-reflection is a powerful tool that complements the manifestation process. In this section, we will explore the relationship between manifestation and self-reflection, understanding the importance of personal growth and self-awareness. We will also discuss the significance of reflecting on past manifestations and the lessons learned from them. Moreover, we will delve into adjusting strategies and intentions as needed to align with your evolving desires. Get ready to deepen your self-awareness and enhance your manifestation journey through the power of self-reflection.

A. Examining Personal Growth and Self-Awareness
Personal growth and self-awareness are crucial aspects of the manifestation process. When you embark on a journey of self-reflection, you gain insights into your beliefs, desires, and

patterns that shape your reality. By examining and understanding yourself on a deeper level, you can identify areas for growth and expansion.

Engage in self-reflection by setting aside dedicated time to introspect. Ask yourself meaningful questions about your values, passions, and aspirations. Explore your strengths and areas for improvement. This process of self-discovery enhances your self-awareness, empowering you to align your manifestations with your authentic self.

B. Reflecting on Past Manifestations and Lessons Learned
Reflecting on past manifestations allows you to glean valuable insights and lessons. Look back on the desires you have already manifested and consider the journey that led you to their fruition. Take note of the thoughts, emotions, and actions that contributed to their manifestation.

Identify the lessons learned from past manifestations. Did you encounter any challenges or obstacles along the way? How did you overcome them? Reflecting on your past manifestations not only highlights your growth but also offers guidance for future manifestations. It helps you identify patterns, strengths, and areas where you can refine your manifestation strategies.

C. Adjusting Strategies and Intentions as Needed
As you engage in self-reflection, you may discover shifts in your desires, values, or priorities. It is essential to adjust your manifestation strategies and intentions accordingly. Embrace the flexibility to refine and realign your approach to match your evolving aspirations.

Consider whether your current strategies and intentions still resonate with your authentic self. Are there any changes you need to make to align with your current vision? Allow yourself the freedom to adjust your course as needed, honoring your growth and the wisdom gained from self-reflection.

Remember that self-reflection is an ongoing process. Continuously assess your desires, beliefs, and alignment with your intentions. Stay attuned to your inner guidance and be open to making adjustments along your manifestation journey. By doing so, you ensure that your manifestations remain aligned with your true self and continue to unfold in harmony with your evolving desires.

Summary

Self-reflection is a powerful tool that complements the manifestation process. By examining personal growth and self-awareness, reflecting on past manifestations and lessons learned, and adjusting strategies and intentions as needed, you deepen your connection with yourself and refine your manifestation journey. Embrace the transformative power of self-reflection, as it guides you to align your desires, beliefs, and actions with your authentic self. So, engage in self-reflection, gain insights, and let your manifestations flourish in harmony with your ever-evolving self.

Part 10: Overcoming Obstacles and Resistance

Obstacles and resistance are common challenges that arise on the path of manifestation. In this section, we will explore the strategies to overcome these hurdles and continue moving forward towards your desires. We will delve into identifying and overcoming resistance, addressing self-doubt and fear of failure, and embracing resilience and perseverance. By understanding how to navigate these obstacles, you can maintain a strong and unwavering focus on manifesting your dreams. So, let's dive in and learn how to overcome obstacles and resistance on your manifestation journey.

A. Identifying and Overcoming Resistance to Manifestation

Resistance often manifests as a series of limiting beliefs, doubts, and negative thought patterns that hinder your manifestation process. To overcome resistance, it is crucial to identify its presence in your life.

Take a moment to observe your thoughts and emotions. Are there any recurring patterns of doubt or self-sabotage? Are there underlying fears or insecurities that are holding you back? By bringing awareness to these resistances, you can consciously choose to release and transcend them.

One effective approach to overcome resistance is through reframing your beliefs. Challenge and replace limiting beliefs with empowering ones that support your manifestation journey. Practice positive affirmations, visualize success, and surround yourself with supportive and like-minded individuals. By consciously choosing thoughts and beliefs that align with your desires, you can dissolve resistance and open the door to unlimited possibilities.

B. Dealing with Self-Doubt and Fear of Failure

Self-doubt and fear of failure can be significant obstacles on the path of manifestation. These emotions often stem from past experiences, societal conditioning, or a fear of stepping outside your comfort zone. It is important to address and overcome these challenges to move forward towards your goals.

Start by acknowledging that self-doubt and fear are normal emotions that arise when you venture into the unknown. Recognize that they are not definitive truths but rather temporary roadblocks that can be overcome. Cultivate self-compassion and remind yourself that everyone experiences doubts and fears.

To overcome self-doubt and fear of failure, focus on the evidence of your capabilities and past successes. Reflect on times when you have overcome challenges and achieved your goals. Celebrate your strengths and talents. Surround yourself with a supportive network that encourages and uplifts you. Embrace a growth mindset that views failures as valuable learning experiences and stepping stones towards success.

C. Embracing Resilience and Perseverance

Resilience and perseverance are essential qualities on the manifestation journey. They empower you to bounce back from setbacks, stay committed to your desires, and persist in the face of challenges.

Embrace resilience by reframing failures as learning opportunities. See them as feedback that guides you towards refinement and growth. Practice self-care to nurture your physical, emotional, and mental well-being. Surround yourself with positive influences and engage in activities that recharge your energy and motivation.

Perseverance is the unwavering determination to continue despite obstacles. Break down your goals into smaller, manageable steps. Celebrate each milestone along the way, no matter how small. Stay focused on the bigger picture and remind yourself of the reasons why you are pursuing your desires.

Summary
Overcoming obstacles and resistance is an integral part of the manifestation journey. By identifying and overcoming resistance, dealing with self-doubt and fear of failure, and embracing resilience and perseverance, you strengthen your ability to manifest your dreams. Remember that obstacles are opportunities for growth and self-discovery. Approach them with determination and a positive mindset. With unwavering focus and a resilient spirit, you can overcome any challenges that come your way and manifest your desires into reality. Stay committed, trust the process, and keep moving forward on your journey to manifestation success.

Part 11: Cultivating a Supportive Environment
Creating a supportive environment is crucial for the manifestation journey. In this section, we will explore the significance of surrounding yourself with positive influences, seeking support from like-minded individuals, and creating an environment that nurtures manifestation. Your surroundings and the people you interact with have a profound impact on your energy, beliefs, and actions. By intentionally cultivating a supportive environment, you enhance your ability to manifest your desires. So, let's delve into the ways to create an environment that uplifts and empowers you on your manifestation path.

A. Surrounding Yourself with Positive Influences
The people and influences around you play a vital role in shaping your mindset and energy. It is essential to surround yourself with positive influences that align with your desires and aspirations. Seek out individuals who uplift, inspire, and believe in your manifestation journey.

Evaluate the relationships in your life and assess how they impact your energy and mindset. Surround yourself with people who support your dreams, offer encouragement, and celebrate your successes. Limit your exposure to negativity and toxic influences that drain your energy and discourage your manifestations.

In addition to the people around you, consider the media you consume. Pay attention to the books, movies, music, and online content that you engage with regularly. Choose uplifting and positive forms of entertainment and information that nourish your mind and spirit.

B. Seeking Support from Like-Minded Individuals

Connecting with like-minded individuals who share your interest in manifestation can be incredibly empowering. Seek out communities, groups, or forums where you can engage with others on the same journey. These like-minded individuals can provide support, guidance, and inspiration along your manifestation path.

Joining a manifestation-focused community allows you to share your experiences, learn from others, and gain new insights. It creates a sense of belonging and camaraderie, as you surround yourself with individuals who understand and support your manifestation endeavors.

Engage in meaningful conversations, attend workshops or seminars, and participate in group activities centered around manifestation. By connecting with like-minded individuals, you expand your knowledge, receive validation, and foster a sense of collective manifestation energy.

C. Creating an Environment that Nurtures Manifestation

Your physical environment plays a significant role in supporting your manifestation journey. Create a space that nurtures and inspires you. Whether it's your home, office, or personal sanctuary, infuse it with elements that align with your desires.

Organize and declutter your physical space to create a sense of harmony and order. Add elements that symbolize your manifestations, such as vision boards, affirmations, or objects that hold personal significance. Surround yourself with colors, scents, and artwork that evoke positive emotions and align with your intentions.

Consider the energetic aspects of your environment as well. Clear the space of any negative or stagnant energy through practices like smudging, cleansing rituals, or energy healing techniques. Infuse your space with positive energy by incorporating natural elements, such as plants, crystals, or natural light.

Summary

Cultivating a supportive environment is a vital aspect of the manifestation journey. Surrounding yourself with positive influences, seeking support from like-minded individuals, and creating an environment that nurtures manifestation enhances your ability to manifest your desires. Choose your relationships and influences consciously, ensuring they align with your goals and aspirations. Seek out communities of like-minded individuals who can support and inspire you. Create a physical environment that reflects and amplifies your intentions. By intentionally cultivating a supportive environment, you create a powerful foundation for manifestation success. So, surround yourself with positivity, seek support, and nurture an environment that uplifts and empowers you on your manifestation journey.

Part 12: Celebrating Manifestation Milestones

Acknowledging and celebrating your manifestation milestones is an essential practice on your journey to creating a life filled with abundance and joy. In this section, we will explore the significance of recognizing and celebrating small victories, the power of gratitude and appreciation, and cultivating a mindset of abundance and joy. By honoring and appreciating the progress you've made, you amplify the positive energy surrounding your manifestations and pave the way for even greater success. So, let's dive into the ways you can celebrate your manifestation milestones along the way.

A. Acknowledging and Celebrating Small Victories

Manifestation is a journey comprised of small steps and milestones. It's important to acknowledge and celebrate each step forward, no matter how small it may seem. Recognizing and celebrating these milestones not only boosts your motivation but also reinforces your belief in the *Power of Manifestation*.

Take time to reflect on your progress and the accomplishments you've achieved. Whether it's a manifestation that has fully materialized or a significant shift in your mindset and actions, celebrate it. Treat yourself to something special, indulge in a favorite activity, or simply take a moment to appreciate and honor the progress you've made.

Remember, every small victory brings you closer to your ultimate goals. By acknowledging and celebrating these milestones, you infuse your manifestation journey with positive energy, confidence, and a sense of achievement.

B. Recognizing the Power of Gratitude and Appreciation

Gratitude and appreciation are powerful tools for manifestation. When you express gratitude for what you've already manifested, you invite more abundance into your life. Take time to appreciate the manifestations, blessings, and experiences that have unfolded along your journey.

Create a gratitude practice by writing in a gratitude journal or simply taking a few moments each day to reflect on the things you're grateful for. As you acknowledge and appreciate the manifestations in your life, you send a clear message to the universe that you are open and receptive to more abundance.

Express your gratitude not only for the desired outcomes but also for the lessons, growth, and synchronicities that have come your way. Embrace a mindset of appreciation, knowing that every step forward is a gift and an opportunity for further expansion.

C. Cultivating a Mindset of Abundance and Joy

Manifestation is not just about achieving specific goals; it's about cultivating a mindset of abundance and joy. Celebrating your manifestation milestones involves embracing an attitude of gratitude and focusing on the abundance that already exists in your life.

Shift your focus from lack to abundance by consciously directing your thoughts and emotions toward joy, appreciation, and positivity. Practice daily affirmations that reinforce your belief in the abundance of the universe and your ability to attract what you desire.

Surround yourself with experiences, people, and activities that bring you joy and align with your desired manifestations. Engage in acts of self-care, indulge in hobbies you love, and make time for activities that fill your heart with happiness.

By cultivating a mindset of abundance and joy, you align your energy with the frequency of your desires. Celebrate each milestone as an affirmation of your power to create a life filled with abundance, joy, and fulfilment.

Summary
Celebrating manifestation milestones is an integral part of the manifestation journey. By acknowledging and celebrating small victories, recognizing the power of gratitude and appreciation, and cultivating a mindset of abundance and joy, you amplify the positive energy surrounding your manifestations. Take time to honor and celebrate your progress, expressing gratitude for what you've already manifested while maintaining a focus on the abundance and joy that lie ahead. Remember, every milestone is a stepping stone on your path to manifestation success. So, celebrate, appreciate, and embrace the abundant and joyous life you are creating through your manifestations.

Conclusion: The Power of Manifestation
Congratulations! You have reached the end of this journey exploring the *Power of Manifestation* and unleashing your inner potential. Throughout this book, we have delved into various aspects of manifestation, understanding the law of attraction, aligning with your desires, visualization techniques, affirmations, and mantras, overcoming limiting beliefs, taking inspired action, cultivating gratitude, practicing patience and trust, self-reflection, overcoming obstacles, cultivating a supportive environment, and celebrating manifestation milestones.

Manifestation is not some mystical or inaccessible concept; it is a powerful tool that is available to every one of us. By understanding the fundamental principles and implementing the strategies discussed in this book, you have gained the knowledge and tools to manifest the life you truly desire.

Remember, manifestation is a journey that requires consistent effort, self-reflection, and belief in your own power. It is about aligning your thoughts, emotions, and actions with your desires, and allowing the universe to respond in kind. The power lies within you to create the reality you envision.

As you continue your manifestation journey, embrace the process with an open mind and heart. Trust in your own abilities and the guidance of the universe. Be patient with yourself and the timing of your manifestations, knowing that everything unfolds in perfect divine order.

Stay connected to your true desires and goals, continually clarifying your intentions and priorities. Embrace a positive mindset, affirming your worthiness and ability to manifest your dreams. Challenge and overcome any limiting beliefs that may arise along the way, replacing them with empowering thoughts and patterns.

Take inspired action, stepping out of your comfort zone and embracing opportunities that come your way. Surround yourself with a supportive environment, seeking like-minded individuals who can uplift and inspire you on your manifestation journey.

Cultivate gratitude as a powerful manifestation tool, appreciating the present moment and the blessings that abound in your life. Let gratitude be the fuel that attracts more abundance and joy into your experience.

Through self-reflection, adjust your strategies and intentions as needed, recognizing your personal growth and the lessons learned along the way. Embrace resilience and perseverance, overcoming obstacles and resistance with unwavering determination.

Finally, remember to celebrate your manifestation milestones, both big and small. Acknowledge your progress, express gratitude for what you have manifested, and cultivate a mindset of abundance and joy. Celebrate the manifestations that have come to fruition, knowing that they are a testament to your power to create.

Now, armed with the knowledge and tools presented in this book, it is time for you to step into your true potential and unleash the *Power of Manifestation* in your life. Trust in yourself and the process, and watch as your dreams and desires become your reality.

May your journey be filled with abundance, joy, and limitless possibilities. Continue to explore, learn, and grow as you unleash your inner potential and manifest a life beyond your wildest dreams.

Remember, the power to manifest is within you. Embrace it, believe in it, and let it guide you towards a life of fulfilment and purpose.

Wishing you an extraordinary manifestation journey ahead!

Chapter 2: Understanding the Law of Attraction: Creating Your Reality

Welcome to 'Understanding the Law of Attraction: Creating Your Reality.' In this chapter, we will delve into the fascinating world of the *Law of Attraction* and explore how it can empower you to shape your own reality. Whether you have just heard about the *Law of Attraction* or have been intrigued by its possibilities for some time, this chapter will provide you with a comprehensive understanding of its principles and how to apply them in your life.

The *Law of Attraction* is not merely a passing fad or a vague concept; it is a powerful tool that can transform your life. By understanding and harnessing the *Law of Attraction*, you gain the ability to consciously create the experiences, circumstances, and outcomes you desire. It is an invitation to take charge of your own destiny and manifest the happiness and fulfilment you deserve.

We will begin by defining what the *Law of Attraction* is and its basic principles. We will delve into the role of thoughts, emotions, and beliefs in the manifestation process, and how they shape our reality. We will also explore the science behind the *Law of Attraction*, examining the relationship between quantum physics and our ability to create our own reality.

Furthermore, we will address the influence of beliefs and subconscious programming on manifestation and provide practical techniques to identify and transform limiting beliefs. Visualization and affirmations will be explored as powerful tools to align with our desires and manifest them into reality. We will also discuss the importance of emotions in the manifestation process and how to cultivate positive emotions to enhance our manifestations.

Taking inspired action will be emphasized as a crucial component of the *Law of Attraction*, as we explore the importance of aligning our actions with our intentions and overcoming obstacles and resistance along the way. We will also delve into the significance of gratitude and appreciation, as well as the art of allowing and letting go, trusting in the process, and surrendering to the universe's wisdom.

Moreover, we will touch upon self-reflection and growth, examining the lessons we can learn from past manifestations and how to adjust our strategies and intentions accordingly. Cultivating a supportive environment will also be explored, emphasizing the importance of surrounding ourselves with positive influences and seeking support from like-minded individuals.

By the end of this chapter, you will have a comprehensive understanding of the *Law of Attraction* and its practical application in your life. So, get ready to unlock the secrets of creating your own reality and embark on a journey of manifestation and personal transformation. Are you ready to take the first step towards creating a happier, more fulfilling life? Let's dive in!

Part 1: What is the Law of Attraction?

Before we dive deeper into understanding the *Law of Attraction*, it's essential to establish a solid foundation of what it is and how it works. In this section, we will explore the definition and basic principles of the *Law of Attraction*, the role of thoughts, emotions, and beliefs in manifestation, and its significance as a universal law.

A. Definition and Basic Principles

The *Law of Attraction* is the belief that like attracts like, and by focusing on positive or negative thoughts, we can bring corresponding experiences into our lives. Simply put, it suggests that we attract what we predominantly think and feel. Our thoughts and emotions act as energetic magnets, drawing similar experiences, circumstances, and people towards us.

At its core, the *Law of Attraction* is based on the principle that everything in the universe is made up of energy, including our thoughts and emotions. This means that we are in constant vibrational resonance with the world around us. Understanding this fundamental principle opens up a world of possibilities, as it means we have the power to consciously direct our energy and shape our reality.

B. The Role of Thoughts, Emotions, and Beliefs in Manifestation

Thoughts, emotions, and beliefs play a crucial role in the *Law of Attraction* and the manifestation process. Our thoughts serve as the starting point, as they generate the energetic vibrations that attract corresponding experiences. When we consistently focus on positive thoughts and maintain a mindset of abundance, we send out a powerful signal to the universe, aligning ourselves with the manifestation of our desires.

However, it is not just our thoughts that shape our reality; our emotions carry significant weight as well. Emotions act as powerful energetic amplifiers, infusing our thoughts with a potent vibrational charge. When we align our thoughts and emotions, we create a powerful magnetic force that draws our desires closer.

Moreover, our beliefs act as filters through which we interpret and perceive the world. If we hold limiting beliefs that contradict our desires, they can act as barriers to manifestation. By identifying and transforming these limiting beliefs, we can remove the blocks that hinder our progress and open ourselves up to new possibilities.

C. Law of Attraction as a Universal Law

The *Law of Attraction* is not just a passing trend or a new-age concept; it is a universal law that operates regardless of our awareness or understanding of it. Similar to the law of gravity, the *Law of Attraction* functions consistently and impartially, responding to the vibrations we emit. It is not something we can turn on or off; it is always in motion, shaping our reality based on the energy we project.

Understanding the *Law of Attraction* empowers us to become conscious creators of our lives. It invites us to take responsibility for our thoughts, emotions, and beliefs, knowing that they directly influence our experiences. By aligning ourselves with the principles of the *Law of*

Attraction, we can harness its power to manifest our desires and create a life filled with happiness, abundance, and fulfilment.

Summary

In this section, we have explored what the *Law of Attraction* is and its basic principles. We have seen how our thoughts, emotions, and beliefs play integral roles in the manifestation process and shape our reality. By understanding the *Law of Attraction* as a universal law, we acknowledge its impartiality and the constant interplay between our energy and the experiences we attract. As we continue our journey of understanding the *Law of Attraction*, let us explore practical techniques and strategies to apply this knowledge in our daily lives.

Part 2: The Power of Thoughts and Energy

In our exploration of understanding the *Law of Attraction*, it is essential to delve into the profound influence that our thoughts and energy have on our reality. This section will uncover the transformative power of thoughts, highlight the vibrational nature of thoughts and emotions, and explain the concept of "like attracts like." By grasping the significance of thoughts and energy, we can harness their potential to manifest our desires and create a life of abundance and fulfilment.

A. How Thoughts Shape Our Reality

Our thoughts serve as the architects of our reality. They are the building blocks that lay the foundation for the experiences we attract. Every thought we think holds a certain energetic frequency, and this energy resonates with the corresponding experiences in the universe. Understanding the *Law of Attraction* reminds us of the power we hold in our thoughts, as they shape our perceptions, decisions, and actions.

When we consistently think positive, empowering thoughts, we generate a magnetic field of optimism and possibility. This energy influences our perceptions, leading us to notice opportunities and solutions that align with our desires. Conversely, negative thoughts carry a lower vibrational frequency, attracting experiences that mirror our fears and limitations. By consciously directing our thoughts towards what we want to create, we take an active role in shaping our reality.

B. Understanding the Vibrational Nature of Thoughts and Emotions

Thoughts and emotions are not static entities; they are dynamic and energetic in nature. Every thought and emotion emits a vibrational frequency that carries a distinct energetic charge. This vibration acts as a powerful magnet, attracting similar vibrations in the external world. By aligning our thoughts and emotions with our desires, we create a harmonious resonance that draws those desires closer to us.

When we experience positive emotions such as joy, gratitude, and love, our vibrational frequency rises, amplifying the manifestation process. These elevated emotions align us with the abundant possibilities present in the universe. On the other hand, negative emotions such as fear, anger, or doubt emit lower vibrational frequencies, hindering the manifestation of our desires.

Understanding the *Law of Attraction* invites us to cultivate awareness of our thoughts and emotions, recognizing their impact on our energetic vibration. By consciously choosing thoughts and emotions that uplift us and align with our desires, we elevate our vibrational frequency, enhancing our ability to attract positive experiences.

C. The Concept of Like Attracts Like

The *Law of Attraction* operates on the principle that "like attracts like." This means that the energy we emit through our thoughts and emotions draws corresponding experiences into our lives. If we consistently dwell on lack and scarcity, we attract more of the same. However, when we focus on abundance, gratitude, and positivity, we attract experiences that reflect those qualities.

This principle highlights the importance of aligning our thoughts, emotions, and beliefs with our desires. By intentionally cultivating positive thoughts and emotions that resonate with what we want to manifest, we create a magnetic pull that brings those desires into our reality. It is not simply wishful thinking; it is an active process of aligning our energy with the energy of what we want to attract.

Understanding the *Law of Attraction* encourages us to become conscious creators of our thoughts and energy. By consistently nurturing positive thoughts, maintaining elevated emotions, and aligning our energy with our desires, we tap into the powerful principle of like attracts like and unlock the door to limitless possibilities.

Summary
In this section, we have explored the profound influence of thought and energy in understanding the *Law of Attraction*. We have seen how thoughts shape our reality, serving as the architects of our experiences. Additionally, we have recognized the vibrational nature of thoughts and emotions and their impact on our ability to manifest our desires. By embracing the concept of like attracts like, we empower ourselves to consciously direct our thoughts and energy toward what we want to attract. As we continue our journey of understanding the *Law of Attraction*, let us explore practical techniques to harness the power of our thoughts and energy and create a life of abundance and fulfilment.

Part 3: The Science Behind the Law of Attraction
In our exploration of understanding the *Law of Attraction*, it is important to examine the scientific aspects that support its principles. This section delves into the intriguing connection between quantum physics and the *Law of Attraction*, explores the impact of thoughts on the energy field, and presents evidence and research that lend credibility to this universal law. By understanding the scientific underpinnings of the *Law of Attraction*, we can further appreciate its potential to shape our reality and manifest our desires.

A. Quantum Physics and the Law of Attraction:
Quantum physics, a branch of science that studies the fundamental nature of matter and energy, offers intriguing insights into the workings of the *Law of Attraction*. At the quantum level, particles and energy exhibit properties that

defy traditional Newtonian physics. Instead, they behave in ways influenced by observation and consciousness.

Quantum theory suggests that our thoughts and intentions have a direct impact on the energy field around us. The observer effect, a phenomenon observed in quantum experiments, suggests that the act of observation influences the behavior and manifestation of particles. Similarly, the *Law of Attraction* proposes that our focused thoughts and intentions can shape the energetic field around us, ultimately influencing the experiences and circumstances we attract.

B. The Impact of Thoughts on the Energy Field
Our thoughts are not merely fleeting mental activities; they generate energy that extends beyond our physical bodies. This energy forms an electromagnetic field that interacts with the energetic fabric of the universe. The *Law of Attraction* acknowledges that our thoughts, particularly when consistently held, emit specific vibrations that resonate with corresponding experiences.

Understanding the *Law of Attraction* invites us to consider the concept of entrainment, which states that vibrations of similar frequencies synchronize over time. When our thoughts consistently align with a specific desire, they create a coherent and powerful energy field that magnetizes experiences in harmony with those thoughts. This phenomenon suggests that our thoughts, through their energetic vibrations, play a significant role in attracting and creating our reality.

C. Evidence and Research Supporting the Law of Attraction
While the *Law of Attraction* is often associated with spiritual and metaphysical teachings, scientific research has shed light on its validity. Although empirical evidence may vary, there are several studies that provide intriguing insights into the workings of this universal law.

Research in the field of positive psychology, for example, has demonstrated the benefits of optimism and positive thinking on well-being and success. Studies on the placebo effect have revealed the influence of beliefs and expectations on healing and medical outcomes. Moreover, studies exploring the power of visualization and mental imagery have shown their effectiveness in enhancing performance and achieving goals.

While more scientific exploration is needed to fully understand the intricacies of the *Law of Attraction*, the existing evidence suggests a correlation between our thoughts, emotions, beliefs, and the outcomes we attract into our lives.

Summary
In this section, we have explored the scientific aspects that support the *Law of Attraction*, further enhancing our understanding of its principles. Quantum physics provides intriguing parallels between the behavior of particles and the influence of consciousness on our reality. We have also recognized the impact of thoughts on the energy field, understanding that our focused thoughts emit vibrations that resonate with corresponding experiences. Additionally, the existing body of research offers insights into the correlation between thoughts, beliefs, and the outcomes we manifest.

By embracing the science behind the *Law of Attraction*, we expand our appreciation for its potential to shape our reality and manifest our desires. As we move forward, let us explore practical techniques and strategies that align with these scientific principles, empowering us to harness the full potential of the *Law of Attraction* in our lives.

Part 4: Beliefs and Subconscious Programming
In our exploration of understanding the *Law of Attraction*, it is crucial to recognize the profound influence of our beliefs and subconscious programming on our ability to manifest our desires. This section delves into the role of beliefs in the manifestation process, provides insights on identifying and transforming limiting beliefs, and offers techniques for reprogramming the subconscious mind to align with success and abundance. By understanding how beliefs and subconscious programming impact the *Law of Attraction*, we can empower ourselves to create the reality we desire.

A. The Influence of Beliefs on Manifestation
Beliefs are the deeply ingrained convictions and assumptions we hold about ourselves, others, and the world around us. They serve as the foundation upon which our thoughts, emotions, and actions are built. Understanding the *Law of Attraction* requires us to acknowledge that our beliefs play a significant role in shaping our reality.

Our beliefs act as filters through which we perceive and interpret the events and circumstances in our lives. If we hold limiting beliefs that contradict our desires, it becomes challenging to manifest them. For instance, if we believe that we are unworthy of success or that abundance is scarce, these beliefs will create a vibrational mismatch with our intentions, hindering the manifestation process.

B. Identifying and Transforming Limiting Beliefs
Identifying our limiting beliefs is a crucial step in the manifestation journey. It requires self-reflection and a willingness to explore the thoughts and patterns that may be holding us back. Pay attention to recurring negative thoughts, self-doubt, and areas of resistance in your life. These can often point to underlying limiting beliefs that need to be addressed.

To transform limiting beliefs, we must challenge their validity and replace them with empowering ones. Start by questioning the evidence and origins of your limiting beliefs. Are they based on past experiences, societal conditioning, or unfounded assumptions? By questioning their validity, we create space for new, empowering beliefs to emerge.

Affirmations, visualization, and daily conscious reprogramming can be powerful tools in replacing limiting beliefs with positive, supportive ones. Surround yourself with positive influences, seek support from like-minded individuals, and immerse yourself in resources that reinforce your desired beliefs. Over time, consistent effort and practice will help rewire your subconscious mind and align it with the success and abundance you seek.

C. Reprogramming the Subconscious Mind for Success and Abundance:

Our subconscious mind plays a significant role in manifesting our desires. It acts as a powerful storehouse of beliefs, emotions, and memories that influence our thoughts and behaviors. To harness the full potential of the *Law of Attraction*, we must reprogram our subconscious mind to support our goals and aspirations.

Reprogramming the subconscious mind involves engaging in practices that bypass the critical conscious mind and directly access the subconscious. Techniques such as hypnosis, guided visualization, and repetition of affirmations can help imprint new beliefs and intentions in the subconscious.

Consistency and repetition are key when reprogramming the subconscious mind. Engage in daily practices that reinforce your desired beliefs and intentions. Surround yourself with positive and supportive environments and immerse yourself in activities and experiences that align with your aspirations. As you persist in these practices, you gradually create new neural pathways and solidify empowering beliefs in your subconscious mind.

Summary

In this section, we have explored the profound influence of beliefs and subconscious programming on the *Law of Attraction*. Our beliefs shape our reality, and identifying and transforming limiting beliefs are crucial steps towards manifesting our desires. By engaging in practices that reprogram the subconscious mind, we can align our thoughts, emotions, and actions with success and abundance.

As we deepen our understanding of the role beliefs and subconscious programming play in the manifestation process, let us remain committed to self-reflection, challenging limiting beliefs, and consistently reinforcing empowering thoughts and intentions. In doing so, we unlock the full potential of the *Law of Attraction* and create a reality that reflects our deepest desires and aspirations.

Part 5: Visualization and Affirmations

In our exploration of understanding the *Law of Attraction*, we come across two powerful techniques that can accelerate the manifestation process: visualization and affirmations. These techniques tap into the power of our thoughts and emotions, helping us align with our desires and manifest them into reality. This section delves into the significance of visualization, the art of creating vivid mental images of our desired outcomes, and the effective use of affirmations to reinforce our beliefs and intentions.

A. Harnessing the Power of Visualization in Manifestation

Visualization is a potent tool that allows us to create a mental representation of our desires. By vividly imagining ourselves already experiencing what we wish to manifest, we engage our senses and emotions, bringing our desires to life in our minds. Visualization serves as a bridge between our current reality and the reality we wish to create.

When practicing visualization, it is essential to engage all our senses. Close your eyes and imagine the details of your desired outcome—the sights, sounds, smells, tastes, and sensations associated with it. As you immerse yourself in the experience, feel the positive emotions that arise. This process sends a powerful signal to the universe, aligning your vibration with your desires and amplifying the manifestation process.

B. Creating Vivid Mental Images of Desired Outcomes

To maximize the effectiveness of visualization, it is crucial to create clear and vivid mental images of our desired outcomes. The more detailed and specific the images, the stronger the impression they leave on our subconscious mind and the universe. Immerse yourself in the experience, allowing your imagination to run wild.

As you visualize, pay attention to the emotions that arise. Emotions infuse our visualizations with energy and intensity, enhancing their manifestation potential. Feel the joy, gratitude, and excitement as if your desires have already manifested. By associating positive emotions with your visualizations, you generate a magnetic field that attracts similar experiences into your reality.

C. Crafting and Using Effective Affirmations to Align with Desires

Affirmations are positive statements that reinforce our beliefs and intentions. They help reprogram our subconscious mind and align our thoughts with our desires. Crafting effective affirmations involves using clear, present-tense language that affirms the reality we want to create. For example, instead of saying, "I will be successful," affirm, "I am successful in all areas of my life."

When using affirmations, repetition is key. Consistently repeat your affirmations, ideally in a relaxed and focused state of mind. This practice reinforces positive beliefs, dissolves limiting beliefs, and aligns your thoughts and emotions with your desires. As you consistently affirm your desired reality, your subconscious mind begins to accept and embrace these new beliefs, attracting corresponding experiences into your life.

Summary

Visualization and affirmations are powerful tools that assist us in understanding the *Law of Attraction* and manifesting our desires. By harnessing the power of visualization, we create a vivid mental picture of our desired outcomes, engaging our senses and emotions. Crafting and using effective affirmations helps reprogram our subconscious mind and align our thoughts and beliefs with our aspirations.

As you integrate visualization and affirmations into your manifestation practice, remember to be consistent, patient, and persistent. Embrace the emotions and sensations associated with your desires, allowing them to fuel your visualizations. Reinforce your positive beliefs through affirmations and let them permeate your subconscious mind.

By practicing visualization and affirmations in alignment with the principles of the *Law of Attraction*, you open yourself to a world of possibilities and empower yourself to consciously create the reality you desire.

Part 6: Emotions and Manifestation

As we continue our journey of understanding the *Law of Attraction*, we come to recognize the profound influence of emotions on the manifestation process. Emotions serve as a powerful guiding force, signaling to the universe the vibrational frequency we are emitting. In this section, we explore the role of emotions in manifestation, the importance of cultivating positive emotions, and the need to release negative emotions and resistance that hinder our desires from manifesting.

A. The Role of Emotions in the Manifestation Process

Emotions play a pivotal role in the manifestation process. They act as an energetic magnet, attracting experiences and circumstances that match their vibrational frequency. When we experience positive emotions such as joy, gratitude, and love, we align ourselves with the essence of our desires. Similarly, when we feel negative emotions like fear, doubt, or frustration, we unintentionally attract experiences that reflect those emotions.

Understanding the *Law of Attraction* involves recognizing that our emotions are a feedback mechanism, providing valuable insights into our vibrational state. By paying attention to how we feel, we gain awareness of the thoughts and beliefs we are holding, which are influencing our reality. Emotions serve as our compass, guiding us towards aligning with our desires or alerting us to the need for inner transformation.

B. Cultivating Positive Emotions for Manifestation Success

To enhance our manifestation success, it is crucial to cultivate positive emotions intentionally. Positive emotions act as powerful fuel for our desires, magnifying their manifestation potential. Engage in activities that bring you joy and happiness, surround yourself with positive influences, and practice gratitude for the blessings in your life.

One effective technique for cultivating positive emotions is through visualization. As you vividly imagine your desired outcomes, immerse yourself in the positive emotions associated with them. Feel the excitement, gratitude, and fulfillment as if your desires have already materialized. By generating and sustaining these positive emotions, you align your vibrational frequency with the reality you wish to create.

C. Releasing Negative Emotions and Resistance

Negative emotions and resistance can hinder the manifestation process, acting as energetic roadblocks to our desires. It is essential to identify and release these emotions to create space for positive manifestations. Acknowledge and accept your negative emotions without judgment, allowing them to be fully felt and processed.

One effective method for releasing negative emotions is through emotional release practices. These can include journaling, meditation, deep breathing exercises, or engaging in physical activities like dancing or engaging in creative expression. Find what works best for you and make it a regular part of your routine to release any emotional baggage that may be weighing you down.

To release resistance, it is vital to identify and address any underlying limiting beliefs that may be causing it. Challenge these beliefs, replace them with positive affirmations, and consciously choose thoughts that support your desires. By doing so, you shift your energetic state and remove the obstacles that impede the flow of manifestation.

Summary

Emotions hold immense power in the manifestation process. Understanding the *Law of Attraction* requires us to become aware of the emotions we are experiencing and intentionally cultivate positive ones. By aligning ourselves with the vibrational frequency of our desires, we attract experiences and circumstances that harmonize with our emotions.

Additionally, releasing negative emotions and resistance is essential for allowing our desires to manifest effortlessly. By acknowledging and releasing negative emotions and addressing limiting beliefs, we create a clear pathway for the universe to bring our desires into fruition.

Embrace the power of your emotions, consciously cultivate positive ones, and release any negativity that stands in the way of your manifestations. By doing so, you empower yourself to co-create a reality filled with joy, abundance, and fulfillment.

Part 7: Taking Inspired Action

In our exploration of understanding the *Law of Attraction*, we come to recognize that while thoughts and emotions play a significant role in manifestation, action is equally crucial. Taking inspired action bridges the gap between our desires and their physical manifestation. In this section, we delve into the importance of action, aligning actions with intentions and desires, and overcoming the common obstacles of procrastination and fear of failure.

A. Importance of Action in the Law of Attraction

The *Law of Attraction* operates in harmony with the principle of cause and effect. It responds to the energetic signals we emit through our thoughts, emotions, and beliefs, but it also requires us to take inspired action. Understanding the *Law of Attraction* means recognizing that we are co-creators of our reality. While the universe conspires to bring our desires to fruition, we must actively participate by taking steps towards their realization.

Action is the catalyst that brings our intentions into the physical realm. It demonstrates our commitment and belief in the manifestation process. By taking action, we send a powerful message to the universe that we are ready to receive and act upon the opportunities that arise.

B. Aligning Actions with Intentions and Desires

To manifest effectively, it is essential to align our actions with our intentions and desires. This means taking deliberate and purposeful steps that resonate with our deepest aspirations. Before taking action, clarify your intentions and visualize the desired outcome. Ask yourself, "What actions can I take that align with my intentions?"

Aligning actions with intentions involves making choices that are congruent with the reality you wish to create. Take proactive steps that move you closer to your goals, whether it's acquiring new knowledge, networking, honing your skills, or taking bold leaps outside your comfort zone. Each action taken from a place of alignment strengthens the energetic momentum towards manifestation.

C. Overcoming Procrastination and Fear of Failure
Procrastination and fear of failure are common obstacles that can hinder our progress in the manifestation journey. These emotions stem from self-doubt, limiting beliefs, or the anticipation of potential setbacks. To overcome them, it is important to cultivate a mindset of trust and resilience.

Understanding the *Law of Attraction* empowers us to embrace inspired action with confidence. Replace self-doubt with self-belief and trust in the process. Break down tasks into manageable steps and create a clear action plan. Celebrate each small achievement along the way, as it reinforces your belief in your ability to manifest your desires.

Addressing the fear of failure requires reframing your perspective. See challenges as opportunities for growth and learning rather than setbacks. Recognize that failure is not a final outcome but a stepping stone towards success. Embrace the lessons learned from any perceived failures and use them to refine your approach.

Summary
Taking inspired action is an integral part of the *Law of Attraction*. It complements our thoughts and emotions, creating a harmonious synergy that propels us towards the manifestation of our desires. By aligning our actions with our intentions and overcoming procrastination and fear of failure, we actively participate in co-creating our reality.

Embrace the power of action, knowing that each step taken brings you closer to your desired outcomes. Trust in the process, believe in your own capabilities, and celebrate the progress you make along the way. Through inspired action, you become an active participant in the manifestation journey, unlocking the full potential of the *Law of Attraction*.

Part 8: Gratitude and Appreciation
In our exploration of understanding the *Law of Attraction*, we come to recognize the profound influence of gratitude and

appreciation in the manifestation process. Cultivating gratitude and embracing appreciation act as powerful catalysts for attracting abundance and aligning with our desires. In this section, we will delve into the significance of gratitude as a manifestation tool, appreciating the present moment and blessings, and how a grateful mindset amplifies abundance.

A. Cultivating Gratitude as a Manifestation Tool

Gratitude is a transformative practice that aligns us with the frequency of abundance. When we express gratitude, we shift our focus from what is lacking to what is already present in our lives. This shift in perspective creates a powerful energetic vibration that attracts more of what we appreciate. Understanding the *Law of Attraction* teaches us that like attracts like, and gratitude acts as a magnetic force, drawing in more blessings and positive experiences.

To cultivate gratitude as a manifestation tool, start by practicing daily gratitude exercises. Take a few moments each day to reflect on the things you are grateful for. Write them down in a gratitude journal or simply express them silently in your mind. Focus on both the big and small blessings in your life, appreciating the abundance that surrounds you. As you consistently practice gratitude, you will notice an expansion of joy and a deepening connection with the flow of manifestation.

B. Appreciating the Present Moment and Blessings

One of the keys to understanding the *Law of Attraction* is recognizing that the present moment is the point of attraction for all that we desire. By fully immersing ourselves in the present and appreciating the blessings that exist here and now, we create fertile ground for the manifestation of our desires. When we live in a state of appreciation, we align ourselves with the abundance that is already available to us.

Take time each day to be fully present and engage with the beauty and wonder around you. Notice the small miracles, the moments of joy, and the acts of kindness. Embrace gratitude for the simple pleasures of life, such as a warm cup of coffee, a loving gesture from a friend, or the beauty of nature. By appreciating the present moment and counting our blessings, we invite more positive experiences into our reality.

C. Amplifying Abundance Through a Grateful Mindset

A grateful mindset serves as a powerful amplifier of abundance. When we approach life with gratitude, we shift our energy from lack to abundance. This shift opens the floodgates of manifestation, attracting more blessings, opportunities, and experiences that align with our desires. Understanding the *Law of Attraction* teaches us that our thoughts and emotions create our reality, and a grateful mindset generates positive thoughts and emotions that magnetize abundance.

To cultivate a grateful mindset, practice reframing challenges as opportunities for growth. Embrace the lessons they offer and express gratitude for the wisdom gained. Surround yourself with reminders of gratitude, such as affirmations, gratitude journals, or vision boards. Engage in acts of kindness and generosity, for they not only bring joy to others but also amplify the abundance in your own life.

Summary

Gratitude and appreciation are essential ingredients in the manifestation process. By cultivating gratitude as a manifestation tool, appreciating the present moment and blessings, and embracing a grateful mindset, we align ourselves with the abundance that the *Law of Attraction* offers. As we deepen our practice of gratitude, we become a magnet for positive experiences, attracting more of what we appreciate and desire. Embrace the power of gratitude and watch as your reality transforms in alignment with your highest intentions and dreams.

Part 9: Allowing and Letting Go

As we continue our journey of understanding the *Law of Attraction*, we come to the profound realization that manifestation is not solely about taking action and exerting control. It also involves the art of allowing and letting go. In this section, we will explore the significance of allowing in the manifestation process, the power of letting go of attachment, and the importance of trusting in divine timing and the unfolding of manifestations.

A. The Art of Allowing in the Manifestation Process

The art of allowing is about creating a space of receptivity and openness for the manifestations we desire. It involves releasing resistance and surrendering to the natural flow of the universe. When we resist or try to force our desires, we create energetic blockages that hinder the manifestation process. Understanding the *Law of Attraction* teaches us that our thoughts, emotions, and beliefs shape our reality. By cultivating an attitude of allowing, we align ourselves with the energy of abundance and create space for our desires to effortlessly come to fruition.

To practice the art of allowing, start by letting go of the need to control every aspect of your manifestations. Instead, trust in the inherent intelligence of the universe and have faith that everything is working in your favor. Cultivate a mindset of abundance and believe that what you desire is already on its way to you. Embrace a sense of ease and flow, knowing that the universe has your back and is conspiring to bring your desires into reality.

B. Letting Go of Attachment and Surrendering to the Universe

Attachment is a common barrier to manifestation. When we cling tightly to specific outcomes and attach our happiness to them, we create resistance and block the natural flow of abundance. Letting go of attachment is a powerful practice that allows us to release control and surrender to the wisdom of the universe. By detaching from the how, when, and where of our desires, we open ourselves up to infinite possibilities and unexpected blessings.

To let go of attachment, cultivate a sense of detachment from the outcome. Focus on the feeling and essence of what you desire rather than getting fixated on the specifics. Trust that the universe knows the best way to bring your desires to fruition and that it may come in ways you cannot yet imagine. Surrender the need to micromanage every step and have faith that everything is unfolding in divine order.

C. Trusting in Divine Timing and the Unfolding of Manifestations

Trusting in divine timing is an essential aspect of the manifestation process. Sometimes, the universe has a grander plan and knows the perfect timing for our desires to manifest. Understanding the *Law of Attraction* involves developing trust in the unseen forces that guide us. When we trust in divine timing, we release the pressure of trying to make things happen on our timeline and allow ourselves to be in sync with the rhythm of the universe.

To cultivate trust in divine timing, practice patience and surrender. Remind yourself that everything is unfolding in perfect order and that there is a higher intelligence at play. Embrace the journey and have faith that the universe is orchestrating the circumstances and synchronicities necessary for your desires to manifest. Trust that the universe has your best interests at heart and that it knows precisely when the time is right for your manifestations to come to fruition.

Summary

Allowing and letting go are integral parts of the manifestation process. By practicing the art of allowing, letting go of attachment, and trusting in divine timing, we create the optimal conditions for our desires to manifest effortlessly. Understanding the *Law of Attraction* invites us to surrender to the flow of the universe, trusting that our desires are being lovingly guided and brought into reality. Embrace the art of allowing, let go with grace, and trust in the unfolding of manifestations. As you do so, watch as the universe beautifully orchestrates the fulfillment of your desires in ways beyond your imagination.

Part 10: Navigating Challenges and Overcoming Resistance

In our exploration of understanding the *Law of Attraction*, we encounter various challenges and resistance that can hinder our manifestation journey. It is essential to equip ourselves with the tools and mindset to navigate these obstacles effectively. In this section, we will delve into recognizing and overcoming obstacles, addressing self-doubt and fear, and cultivating resilience and persistence to stay aligned with our desires.

A. Recognizing and Overcoming Obstacles in Manifestation
On the path of manifestation, obstacles may arise that test our resolve and commitment. It is crucial to recognize these challenges as opportunities for growth and learning rather than roadblocks. Understanding the *Law of Attraction* teaches us that our thoughts and beliefs shape our reality, including the obstacles we encounter. By shifting our perspective and seeing challenges as temporary setbacks, we empower ourselves to overcome them.

To overcome obstacles, start by identifying the limiting beliefs or thought patterns that may be contributing to the challenges. Take a moment to reflect on any negative or self-sabotaging thoughts that arise. Then, consciously replace them with empowering and positive thoughts. Focus on solutions rather than dwelling on the problems. Remember, every obstacle is an invitation for growth and an opportunity to align with your desires on a deeper level.

B. Dealing with Self-Doubt and Fear
Self-doubt and fear can be significant barriers to manifestation. They often stem from past experiences, societal conditioning, or a lack of self-belief. However, understanding the *Law of Attraction* reminds us that we have the power to change our thoughts and beliefs. It is essential to address and transform self-doubt and fear to maintain alignment with our desires.

To deal with self-doubt and fear, practice self-awareness and mindfulness. Notice when self-doubt or fear arises and acknowledge it without judgment. Then, challenge these negative thoughts by focusing on evidence of your capabilities and past successes. Affirmations can also be helpful in reprogramming the subconscious mind and instilling confidence. Surround yourself with positive influences and support and remind yourself that you are worthy of your desires. Cultivate self-compassion and treat yourself with kindness as you navigate through any doubts or fears that may arise.

C. Developing Resilience and Persistence

Resilience and persistence are vital qualities on the path of manifestation. They enable us to stay committed to our desires even in the face of challenges and setbacks. Understanding the *Law of Attraction* requires us to cultivate a mindset of unwavering belief and determination.

To develop resilience and persistence, practice perseverance in the face of adversity. Embrace setbacks as learning opportunities and remain focused on your vision. Surround yourself with supportive and like-minded individuals who can provide encouragement and inspiration. Break down your goals into smaller, manageable steps, and celebrate each milestone along the way. Cultivate a growth mindset, viewing challenges as stepping stones to success rather than insurmountable barriers. Stay committed to your desires, and trust that the universe is conspiring to bring them to fruition.

Summary

As we deepen our understanding of the *Law of Attraction*, we realize that challenges and resistance are an inherent part of the manifestation journey. By recognizing and overcoming obstacles, addressing self-doubt and fear, and cultivating resilience and persistence, we empower ourselves to stay aligned with our desires. Embrace challenges as opportunities for growth, transform self-doubt into self-belief, and develop the resilience to persist in the pursuit of your dreams. Remember, understanding the *Law of Attraction* is not just about attracting what you desire; it is also about nurturing your inner strength and navigating the path to manifesting your reality.

Part 11: Self-Reflection and Growth

As we continue our journey of understanding the *Law of Attraction*, it is crucial to recognize the role of self-reflection and growth in our manifestation process. Self-reflection allows us to gain deeper insights into ourselves, our desires, and the patterns that influence our reality. By learning from past experiences and manifestations, we can adjust our strategies and intentions to align more effectively with our desires. In this section, we will explore the importance of self-reflection, the lessons we can learn from our manifestations, and the significance of adjusting our approach along the way.

A. The Role of Self-Reflection in Manifestation

Self-reflection serves as a powerful tool for understanding the *Law of Attraction*. By taking the time to pause and introspect, we gain valuable insights into our thoughts, emotions, and beliefs. It allows us to become aware of any patterns or blocks that may be hindering our manifestation process. Self-reflection provides an opportunity to examine our intentions, desires, and the alignment between our inner world and outer manifestations.

Engage in regular self-reflection by setting aside dedicated time for introspection. Find a quiet space where you can be alone with your thoughts. Reflect on your current manifestations and ask yourself questions such as: What beliefs or emotions are influencing my reality? Are there any patterns or recurring themes in my manifestations? Am I fully aligned with my desires? By honestly and objectively examining your thoughts and actions, you can gain valuable insights that guide you towards manifestation success.

B. Learning from Past Experiences and Manifestations

Our past experiences and manifestations are rich sources of wisdom and learning. Each manifestation, whether perceived as successful or unsuccessful, provides us with valuable feedback and insights. Understanding the *Law of Attraction* involves being open to learning from our past and embracing the lessons they offer.

Take time to review your past manifestations. Reflect on the outcomes, the journey, and the lessons learned along the way. Ask yourself: What worked well? What could be improved? Did any limiting beliefs or doubts arise? By recognizing the patterns and connections between your thoughts, emotions, and outcomes, you can refine your approach and make conscious adjustments. Embrace the lessons learned and carry them forward as you continue your manifestation journey.

C. Adjusting Strategies and Intentions as Needed
Flexibility and adaptability are essential when it comes to understanding the *Law of Attraction*. As you gain insights through self-reflection and learn from your past experiences, be open to adjusting your strategies and intentions accordingly. The manifestation process is not set in stone; it requires us to be responsive and open to change.

If you notice that certain strategies or intentions are not yielding the desired results, be willing to adjust them. Revisit your beliefs, thoughts, and emotions surrounding your desires. Are there any areas where you can refine or strengthen your alignment? Be open to exploring new approaches, techniques, or perspectives that resonate with you. Remember, manifestation is a co-creative process with the universe, and it is essential to adapt as you grow and evolve.

Summary
Self-reflection and growth play a significant role in our understanding of the *Law of Attraction*. Through self-reflection, we gain valuable insights into our thoughts, emotions, and beliefs, allowing us to align more effectively with our desires. Learning from past experiences and manifestations provides us with wisdom and guidance for refining our approach. Adjusting our strategies and intentions as needed keeps us in sync with our evolving desires and helps us stay aligned with the flow of manifestation. Embrace self-reflection as a powerful tool for growth, learn from your past, and be open to making adjustments along your manifestation journey. By cultivating self-awareness and adapting your approach, you empower yourself to manifest your dreams with greater clarity and intention.

Part 12: Cultivating a Supportive Environment
As we delve deeper into understanding the *Law of Attraction*, we come to realize that our environment plays a crucial role in our manifestation journey. Creating a supportive environment can greatly enhance our ability to align with our desires and cultivate a positive mindset. In this section, we will explore the importance of surrounding ourselves with positive influences, seeking support from like-minded

individuals, and creating an environment that nurtures happiness and manifestation.

A. Surrounding Yourself with Positive Influences
The people and influences in our lives have a significant impact on our energy, mindset, and overall well-being. To fully harness the power of the *Law of Attraction*, it is essential to surround yourself with positive influences that uplift and inspire you.

Evaluate the relationships and connections in your life. Are they supportive and nurturing? Do they encourage your growth and manifestation journey? Surround yourself with individuals who radiate positivity, share similar goals, and support your dreams. Engage in activities, read books, or listen to podcasts that inspire and motivate you. By immersing yourself in a positive environment, you create a fertile ground for manifestation and align yourself with higher vibrational energies.

B. Seeking Support from Like-Minded Individuals
The journey of understanding the *Law of Attraction* can be more enriching and fulfilling when shared with like-minded individuals. Seek out communities, groups, or forums where you can connect with others who are on a similar path of manifestation and personal growth.

Engage in discussions, share your experiences, and learn from others' insights. Surrounding yourself with like-minded individuals provides a supportive network where you can find encouragement, inspiration, and guidance. Collaborate on projects, participate in manifestation exercises together, and celebrate each other's successes. Together, you can amplify the power of manifestation through collective energy and shared intentions.

C. Creating an Environment that Nurtures Happiness and Manifestation
The physical environment we inhabit also plays a significant role in our manifestation journey. Creating a space that nurtures happiness and supports manifestation can have a

profound impact on our thoughts, emotions, and overall well-being.

Design your surroundings to reflect the energy and intentions you wish to manifest. Declutter and organize your physical space to create a sense of harmony and clarity. Infuse your environment with elements that evoke joy and inspiration, such as uplifting artwork, plants, or meaningful objects. Establish a dedicated space for meditation, visualization, or manifestation rituals. Surround yourself with affirmations, vision boards, or reminders of your goals to reinforce your intentions and keep them at the forefront of your mind.

Summary
Understanding the *Law of Attraction* encompasses not only our internal processes but also the external factors that shape our experiences. Cultivating a supportive environment is vital to harnessing the full potential of manifestation. Surround yourself with positive influences that uplift and inspire you, seek support from like-minded individuals who share your goals, and create a physical environment that nurtures happiness and manifestation. By consciously curating your environment, you align yourself with the energies of abundance and joy, amplifying your manifestation power. Embrace the power of a supportive environment as you continue your journey of understanding the *Law of Attraction* and manifesting your desires with clarity and intention.

Conclusion: Understanding the Law of Attraction
Throughout this article, we have explored the fascinating world of understanding the *Law of Attraction* and its profound impact on creating our reality. We have delved into key concepts and insights, discovering how our thoughts, emotions, beliefs, and actions shape our experiences. Now, as we conclude our exploration, let us recap the key concepts, find encouragement to apply the principles of the *Law of Attraction*, and reflect on the next steps of our journey towards happiness and manifestation success.

In our journey to understand the *Law of Attraction*, we have learned that it is a powerful universal law that states that like attracts like. Our thoughts, emotions, beliefs, and actions emit vibrational frequencies that attract corresponding experiences into our lives. By consciously aligning our thoughts, emotions, and beliefs with our desires, we can manifest the reality we envision.

We discovered the importance of thought and energy in the manifestation process. Our thoughts shape our reality, and by cultivating positive and empowering thoughts, we can create a foundation for manifestation success. We explored the vibrational nature of thoughts and emotions, understanding that they emit energetic frequencies that attract similar frequencies into our lives. By focusing on positive thoughts and emotions, we can magnetize the experiences we desire.

We explored the scientific underpinnings of the *Law of Attraction*, discovering its connections to quantum physics and the impact of our thoughts on the energy field. We encountered evidence and research supporting its validity, strengthening our belief in its power.

We delved into the influence of beliefs on manifestation, recognizing the significance of identifying and transforming limiting beliefs. By reprogramming our subconscious mind with empowering beliefs, we open ourselves to the limitless possibilities of success and abundance.

We explored visualization and affirmations as powerful tools to align with our desires. Through vivid mental imagery and the crafting of effective affirmations, we can strengthen our manifestation practice and create a clear pathway towards our goals.

We acknowledged the role of emotions in the manifestation process and learned to cultivate positive emotions to amplify our manifestation success. By releasing negative emotions and resistance, we create space for positive experiences to flow into our lives.

We recognized the importance of taking inspired action, aligning our actions with our intentions and desires. By overcoming procrastination and fear of failure, we propel ourselves forward on the path of manifestation.

We explored the transformative power of gratitude and appreciation, understanding how cultivating these qualities can amplify abundance and attract more positive experiences into our lives.

We discussed the art of allowing and letting go, surrendering to the universe and trusting in divine timing. By releasing attachment and resistance, we open ourselves to the flow of manifestations and embrace the unfolding of our desires.

We emphasized the role of self-reflection and growth in the manifestation journey. Learning from past experiences, adjusting our strategies, and developing resilience are essential elements of continuous manifestation success.

Lastly, we explored the significance of cultivating a supportive environment, surrounding ourselves with positive influences, seeking support from like-minded individuals, and creating a space that nurtures happiness and manifestation.

Understanding the *Law of Attraction* is just the beginning of our journey towards creating our reality. As we have explored the various concepts and insights, it is crucial to apply these principles in our daily lives. Take what you have learned and put it into practice. Embrace the power of your thoughts, emotions, beliefs, and actions to manifest the life you desire.

Remember that manifestation is a process that requires patience, persistence, and consistent effort. Believe in yourself and your ability to create your reality. Stay focused on your goals, align your thoughts and emotions with your desires, and take inspired action towards your dreams.

Understanding the *Law of Attraction* is an ongoing journey of self-discovery and personal growth. As you continue to explore and apply these principles, trust that you are on the path to happiness and manifestation success. Embrace the process, be open to learning and adjusting along the way, and celebrate even the smallest manifestations as signs of your progress.

Remember to be kind to yourself throughout this journey. Manifestation is not about perfection but about progress.

Allow yourself to learn, grow, and evolve. Surround yourself with positivity, seek support from like-minded individuals, and create an environment that nurtures your manifestation practice.

As you conclude this post, take a moment to reflect on your next steps. Set clear intentions, visualize your desired reality, and take inspired action towards your goals. Trust in the power of the *Law of Attraction*, for you have the ability to create a life filled with joy, abundance, and fulfillment.

Wishing you a transformative journey on the path of understanding the *Law of Attraction* and the manifestation of your dreams. May you embrace your innate power and create a reality that surpasses your wildest dreams.

Chapter 3: The Art of Visualization: Painting Your Dreams into Existence

Welcome to "The Art of Visualization: Painting Your Dreams into Existence." In this chapter, we will explore the transformative power of visualization and how it can help you manifest your dreams and create a happier, more fulfilling life. Whether you are familiar with the Law of Attraction or just beginning to discover its potential, understanding and harnessing the *Art of Visualization* is a key step towards unlocking your inner creative power.

The Law of Attraction teaches us that our thoughts, beliefs, and emotions have a profound influence on the reality we experience. By understanding and applying the principles of the Law of Attraction, we can deliberately shape our lives and manifest our deepest desires. Visualization, as a powerful tool within the Law of Attraction, allows us to harness the creative energy of our thoughts and direct it towards the realization of our dreams.

In this chapter, we will embark on a journey to explore the intricacies of visualization and its role in manifesting our desires. We will delve into the process of visualization, discovering how it works, and why it is an essential practice for anyone seeking to paint their dreams into existence. We will explore the power of mental imagery and the techniques that can help us create compelling visualizations that ignite our passion and motivation.

Furthermore, we will examine how visualization can be used as a manifestation tool, aligning our intentions with the universal flow of energy and abundance. We will learn how to overcome challenges and limiting beliefs that may hinder our visualization practice, empowering ourselves to create a clear and vivid vision of the life we want to lead.

Moreover, we will explore the integration of visualization into our daily lives, finding practical ways to incorporate this transformative practice into our routines and rituals. We will also explore advanced techniques and practices that can take our visualization skills to new heights, amplifying our manifestation potential.

Throughout this chapter, we will be inspired by real-life case studies and success stories, witnessing the transformative effects of visualization in the lives of individuals who have dared to dream big and turned their dreams into reality.

So, if you are ready to tap into your imagination, unleash your creative power, and bring your dreams to life, join us as we embark on this enlightening exploration of "The Art of Visualization: Painting Your Dreams into Existence." Get ready to immerse yourself in the world of visualization, where the canvas of your mind becomes the blueprint for the extraordinary life you deserve.

Part 1: Understanding Visualization

Before we dive into the wonderful world of visualization, let's take a moment to understand its essence and significance. Visualization is not just about daydreaming or wishful thinking; it is a powerful technique that can help us bring our dreams and desires into reality. In this section, we will explore the fundamental aspects of understanding visualization and its profound impact on our lives.

A. Definition and Purpose of Visualization

Visualization can be described as the art of creating vivid mental images or scenes in our mind's eye. It involves using our imagination to construct detailed representations of our desires, goals, and aspirations. By engaging our senses and emotions in this imaginative process, we can bring our visions to life and make them feel real and tangible. The purpose of visualization is to harness the power of our thoughts and tap into the creative energy within us to manifest our dreams.

B. The Connection Between Visualization and Manifestation
Visualization and manifestation go hand in hand. Visualization acts as a bridge between our inner world of thoughts and the outer world of experiences. When we visualize, we are essentially sending a clear and focused message to the universe about what we want to attract into our lives. By consistently immersing ourselves in these visualized experiences, we align our energy with our desires and create a magnetic attraction towards them. Visualization acts as a catalyst for manifestation, helping us materialize our dreams by bringing them from the realm of imagination into physical reality.

C. How Visualization Affects Our Subconscious Mind
Our subconscious mind plays a crucial role in the manifestation process, as it holds our beliefs, attitudes, and deeply ingrained patterns of thinking. Visualization acts as a direct channel to our subconscious mind, bypassing the filters of doubt and limitation. When we vividly imagine our desires as already fulfilled, we are effectively reprogramming our subconscious beliefs and replacing any negative or limiting thoughts with positive and empowering ones. The power of visualization lies in its ability to influence our subconscious mind and shape our perception of what is possible, ultimately paving the way for the manifestation of our dreams.

Summary
Understanding the *Art of Visualization* is a key component of harnessing our innate creative power and manifesting our dreams. By defining visualization and recognizing its purpose, we establish a solid foundation for the transformative journey ahead. We have explored the deep connection between visualization and manifestation, understanding how visualization acts as a powerful magnet that draws our desires closer to us. Furthermore, we have discovered how visualization can reshape our subconscious mind,

reprogramming it with empowering beliefs that support our manifestation journey.

Now that we have laid the groundwork of understanding visualization, we are ready to explore the techniques, strategies, and practical applications that will enhance our visualization skills. So, let's embark on this exciting adventure into the *Art of Visualization*, where the canvas of our imagination becomes the catalyst for turning dreams into reality.

Part 2: The Process of Visualization

Now that we have a solid understanding of visualization, let's dive deeper into the process itself. In this section, we will explore the essential steps and techniques that will enhance your ability to manifest your dreams through the *Art of Visualization*. By setting clear intentions, creating a supportive environment, and utilizing effective visualization techniques, you will be well on your way to painting your dreams into existence.

A. Setting Clear Intentions and Goals

Before we embark on the journey of visualization, it is crucial to have a clear understanding of what we want to manifest. Setting clear intentions and goals provides a sense of direction and focus for our visualization practice. Take some time to reflect on your desires and aspirations, and then clearly define what you want to visualize. The more specific and detailed your intentions and goals are, the easier it becomes to create a vivid mental image that resonates with your desires.

B. Creating a Conducive Environment for Visualization

Creating a supportive environment can greatly enhance the effectiveness of your visualization practice. Find a quiet and comfortable space where you can relax and be free from distractions. Dim the lights, play soothing music if desired, and create an atmosphere that promotes a sense of tranquility and inner focus. You may also consider incorporating elements that inspire and uplift you, such as candles, crystals, or meaningful objects. Designing an environment that aligns with your personal preferences and cultivates a positive and peaceful atmosphere will amplify the power of your visualization practice.

C. Techniques for Effective Visualization

There are several techniques that can enhance the effectiveness of your visualization practice. Experiment with different approaches and find what resonates with you. Here are a few techniques to consider:

1. Guided visualization: This technique involves listening to pre-recorded guided visualizations or using visualization scripts to lead you through a specific visualization journey. Guided visualizations can help you stay focused, provide structure, and deepen your experience.
2. Visualization with affirmations: Combining affirmations with visualization can be a potent practice. As you visualize your desired outcome, repeat positive affirmations that reinforce your belief in the manifestation of your dreams. This combination strengthens the impact of both techniques, aligning your thoughts, emotions, and intentions.
3. Vision boards: Creating a vision board is a visual representation of your desires and goals. Gather images, words, and symbols that represent what you want to manifest and arrange them on a board. Place your vision board in a prominent place where you can see it daily, allowing it to serve as a visual reminder and source of inspiration.

Summary

Mastering the process of visualization is a key aspect of manifesting your dreams through the *Art of Visualization*. By setting clear intentions and goals, creating a conducive environment, and employing effective visualization techniques, you empower yourself to bring your desires into reality. Remember, the *Art of Visualization* is a deeply personal and creative practice. Explore various techniques, adapt them to suit your preferences, and allow your imagination to soar. As you continue on this journey, you will discover the transformative power that lies within you to paint your dreams into existence through the *Art of Visualization*.

Part 3: The Power of Mental Imagery

In the realm of visualization, the power of mental imagery holds immense potential for manifesting our dreams. The ability to create vivid mental images is at the core of the *Art of Visualization*. By harnessing the power of our imagination and engaging our senses, we can enhance the effectiveness of our visualization practice and bring our desires to life. In this section, we will explore the transformative power of mental imagery and how it can amplify the *Art of Visualization*.

A. Using Vivid Mental Images to Enhance Visualization

The essence of visualization lies in the ability to create clear and detailed mental images of our desired outcomes. When we engage our imagination and form vivid mental pictures, we activate the creative forces within us. Visualize yourself already living your dream life, experiencing it in the present moment. See the colors, shapes, and textures. Imagine the sights, sounds, and even the scents associated with your desired reality. The more vivid and realistic you make these mental images, the stronger the impression they create on your subconscious mind. This heightened level of detail helps to solidify your intentions and brings your visualizations to life.

B. Incorporating Sensory Details for a More Immersive Experience

To deepen the impact of your visualization practice, go beyond visual imagery and engage your other senses. Imagine the sensations that accompany the fulfillment of your desires. How does it feel? Is there a particular taste or texture? By incorporating sensory details, such as touch, taste, smell, and sound, you create a more immersive and realistic experience within your mind. This multi-sensory approach activates a wider range of neural pathways, intensifying the emotional connection to your visualizations.

C. Harnessing the Emotional Impact of Visualization

Emotions are the fuel that propels manifestation, and visualization is a potent tool for evoking powerful emotions.

As you engage in your visualizations, allow yourself to fully immerse in the positive emotions associated with your desired reality. Feel the joy, excitement, and gratitude as if your dreams have already come true. Emotions are the language of the subconscious mind, and when combined with vivid mental imagery, they become a magnetic force that attracts your desires into your life. Embrace the positive emotions that arise during your visualizations and let them infuse every aspect of your being.

Summary
The power of mental imagery in the *Art of Visualization* cannot be overstated. By using vivid mental images, incorporating sensory details, and harnessing the emotional impact of visualization, you unlock the full potential of this transformative practice. Allow your imagination to soar, painting vibrant pictures in your mind, and infuse them with the rich tapestry of sensory experiences. As you immerse yourself in the world of your visualizations, you activate the creative forces within you and align yourself with the manifestation of your dreams. The *Art of Visualization*, combined with the power of mental imagery, becomes a potent catalyst for bringing your desires into existence. Embrace the incredible power of your mind and watch as your dreams unfold before your eyes through the *Art of Visualization*.

Part 4: Visualization for Goal Achievement

In the *Art of Visualization*, its application to goal achievement is a powerful tool for turning our dreams into reality. By employing visualization techniques that are tailored to our specific goals, we can create a roadmap for success and motivate ourselves to take the necessary actions. In this section, we will delve into the practical aspects of visualization for goal achievement, exploring how it can help us clarify our objectives, visualize the necessary steps, and serve as a potent source of motivation.

A. Applying Visualization Techniques to Specific Goals

To make the most of the *Art of Visualization*, it is essential to align it with your specific goals. Take some time to clearly define your objectives and understand what you truly desire to achieve. Once you have a clear goal in mind, visualize it as if it has already been accomplished. See yourself in the desired situation, experiencing the emotions and sensations that come with achieving your goal. By vividly picturing your desired outcome, you activate your subconscious mind and set the stage for its manifestation.

B. Visualizing the Steps and Actions Required for Success
Visualization goes beyond merely imagining the end result; it can also be used to visualize the necessary steps and actions that lead to success. Picture yourself engaging in the specific activities that will propel you towards your goal. See yourself taking focused and inspired action, overcoming obstacles, and making progress. By visualizing the process, you create a mental blueprint that guides your actions and helps you stay on track. Visualization becomes a powerful tool for planning and executing the necessary steps to achieve your goals.

C. Using Visualization as a Motivational Tool
Visualization is not only a means to an end but also a potent source of motivation. As you immerse yourself in the *Art of Visualization*, connect with the emotions of accomplishment, satisfaction, and fulfillment that arise from achieving your goals. Let these positive emotions fuel your motivation and drive to take consistent action. By regularly revisiting your visualizations, you reinforce your commitment to your goals and keep your motivation alive. Visualization becomes a dynamic force that propels you forward, even when faced with challenges or setbacks.

Summary
Visualization for goal achievement is a dynamic and practical application of the *Art of Visualization*. By applying visualization techniques to specific goals, visualizing the necessary steps and actions, and using visualization as a motivational tool, you harness the transformative power of your mind to manifest your aspirations. The *Art of Visualization* becomes a personal roadmap for success, guiding your actions and igniting your motivation. So, take the time to visualize your goals with clarity, immerse yourself in the process, and let the power of visualization propel you towards the realization of your dreams. Embrace the *Art of*

Visualization and witness the magic of turning your goals into tangible achievements.

Part 5: Overcoming Challenges in Visualization

While the *Art of Visualization* can be a powerful tool for achieving our goals, it is not without its challenges. In this section, we will explore some common obstacles that may arise during the visualization process and discuss strategies for overcoming them. By addressing skepticism and doubt, challenging limiting beliefs, and enhancing focus and concentration, we can navigate these challenges and fully harness the transformative power of visualization.

A. Dealing with Skepticism and Doubt

When it comes to visualization, skepticism and doubt can hinder our progress. It's natural for doubts to arise, questioning the effectiveness of visualization or our ability to manifest our desires. However, it's important to recognize that visualization is a proven technique used by countless successful individuals. To overcome skepticism, educate yourself about the science behind visualization and learn about the success stories of others who have applied the *Art of Visualization* in their lives. Embrace a mindset of curiosity and open-mindedness, allowing yourself to explore the possibilities without judgment.

B. Addressing Limiting Beliefs and Self-Sabotage

Limiting beliefs and self-sabotage can be significant barriers to successful visualization. These beliefs are often deeply ingrained and can undermine our efforts to manifest our goals. To address this, it's crucial to identify and challenge these limiting beliefs. Engage in self-reflection and examine the beliefs that may be holding you back. Replace negative or self-defeating thoughts with positive and empowering ones. Affirmations can be a helpful tool in reshaping your beliefs. By consistently affirming positive statements about yourself and your abilities, you can gradually reprogram your subconscious mind and overcome self-sabotage.

C. Enhancing Focus and Concentration During Visualization

Maintaining focus and concentration during visualization is essential for maximizing its effectiveness. In our fast-paced and distracting world, it can be challenging to quiet the mind and fully immerse ourselves in the visualization process. To enhance focus, find a quiet and comfortable space where you can engage in uninterrupted visualization. Consider incorporating relaxation techniques, such as deep breathing or meditation, to calm the mind and promote concentration. Additionally, using visual aids, such as vision boards or guided visualization recordings, can help direct your attention and deepen your experience.

Summary

Overcoming challenges in visualization is an integral part of mastering the *Art of Visualization*. By dealing with skepticism and doubt, addressing limiting beliefs and self-sabotage, and enhancing focus and concentration, we can overcome these obstacles and unlock the full potential of visualization. Remember that visualization is a practice that requires patience and persistence. Embrace the process with an open mind, challenge your limiting beliefs, and cultivate a focused mindset. As you navigate these challenges, you will strengthen your ability to harness the power of visualization and manifest your dreams with clarity and intention. Embrace the *Art of Visualization*, overcome the challenges, and witness the transformative impact it can have on your life.

Part 6: Integrating Visualization into Daily Life

To truly harness the transformative power of visualization, it is important to integrate this practice into our daily lives. By incorporating visualization into our morning and evening routines, utilizing it during meditation and relaxation practices, and finding creative ways to infuse it throughout the day, we can maximize its impact and create a more intentional and fulfilling life. In this section, we will explore practical strategies for seamlessly integrating the *Art of Visualization* into our daily routines.

A. Incorporating Visualization into Morning and Evening Routines

Our morning and evening routines provide the perfect opportunity to set the tone for our day and reflect on our progress. By incorporating visualization into these routines, we can align our mindset and intentions with our desired outcomes. In the morning, take a few moments to visualize your day ahead, visualizing success, happiness, and positivity in various areas of your life. In the evening, use visualization to review your day, celebrating your accomplishments and envisioning an even brighter future. By consistently practicing visualization during these key moments, you create a powerful foundation for manifestation.

B. Using Visualization During Meditation and Relaxation Practices

Meditation and relaxation practices offer a serene space for deep introspection and inner growth. By integrating visualization into these practices, we can enhance their effectiveness and tap into our subconscious mind. During meditation, incorporate guided visualizations that align with your goals and aspirations. Envision yourself already achieving what you desire, engaging all your senses to create a vivid mental experience. Use visualization to relax your mind, release stress, and cultivate a sense of peace and tranquility. By merging visualization with meditation and relaxation, you can strengthen your mind-body connection and deepen your manifestation practice.

C. Finding Creative Ways to Integrate Visualization Throughout the Day

While morning and evening routines and meditation sessions provide dedicated times for visualization, we can also find creative ways to infuse it throughout the day. Consider creating visual reminders, such as vision boards or affirmations, that you can place in prominent locations. Take a few moments during breaks or quiet moments to visualize your goals and desires. Use visualization during physical activities like exercise or chores, allowing your mind to explore and manifest while your body is engaged in the task at hand. By finding unique and personalized ways to integrate visualization into your daily life, you cultivate a constant connection to your dreams and aspirations.

Summary

Integrating visualization into our daily lives is key to harnessing the full potential of the *Art of Visualization*. By incorporating it into our morning and evening routines, infusing it into meditation and relaxation practices, and finding creative ways to integrate it throughout the day, we create a consistent and powerful manifestation practice. Visualization becomes a natural part of our mindset and helps us align our thoughts, beliefs, and actions with our desired outcomes. Embrace the *Art of Visualization* as a transformative tool and discover the profound impact it can have on every aspect of your life. Integrate visualization into your daily routine and watch as your dreams paint themselves into existence.

Part 7: Visualization and Emotional Well-Being
Visualization is not only a powerful tool for manifesting our goals and desires but also for enhancing our emotional well-being. By harnessing the *Art of Visualization*, we can actively engage in emotional healing, cultivate positive emotions, and envision a happier and more fulfilling life. In this section, we will explore how visualization can positively impact our emotional state and provide practical techniques to incorporate into our practice.

A. Harnessing Visualization for Emotional Healing and Release
Visualization can be a transformative tool for processing and healing emotions. Through visualization, we can create a safe space within our minds to explore and release negative emotions that may be holding us back. Take time during your visualization practice to identify and visualize the emotions you wish to heal. Imagine them leaving your body and being replaced by feelings of peace, love, and forgiveness. Visualize yourself letting go of past hurts and embracing emotional freedom. The *Art of Visualization* can help us navigate the complexities of our emotions and facilitate a profound healing process.

B. Cultivating Positive Emotions Through Visualization
Visualization is not limited to healing; it can also serve as a powerful catalyst for cultivating positive emotions. By consciously visualizing and immersing ourselves in positive experiences, we can evoke corresponding emotions within us. Choose uplifting and joyful scenarios to visualize, such as

achieving your goals, spending time with loved ones, or basking in moments of success and happiness. Engage all your senses to create a vivid and immersive experience in your mind. As you visualize, allow yourself to feel the positive emotions associated with these experiences, such as joy, gratitude, and fulfillment. By consistently practicing positive visualization, you can reprogram your mind to naturally attract and embody these emotions in your daily life.

C. Visualizing a Happier and More Fulfilling Life
One of the most profound aspects of the *Art of Visualization* is its ability to help us envision and manifest a happier and more fulfilling life. Take time during your visualization practice to create a detailed mental picture of the life you desire. Visualize yourself living with purpose, abundance, and fulfillment. Imagine the specific details of your ideal life—the relationships, career, health, and experiences that bring you joy. Engage your emotions and truly believe in the possibility of this vision becoming your reality. By consistently visualizing your desired life, you align your energy and actions with your aspirations, paving the way for their manifestation.

Summary
Visualization is a remarkable tool that not only helps us manifest our goals but also nurtures our emotional well-being. By harnessing the *Art of Visualization*, we can actively engage in emotional healing and release, cultivate positive emotions, and visualize a happier and more fulfilling life. The power of visualization lies in its ability to tap into the depths of our subconscious mind, align our emotions with our desires, and shape our reality. Embrace the *Art of Visualization* as a means to enhance your emotional well-being and create the life you envision. By immersing yourself in the practice of visualization, you can harness its transformative power and paint a vibrant and emotionally fulfilling canvas of your life.

Part 8: Visualization as a Manifestation Tool
Visualization is a powerful manifestation tool that can accelerate our journey towards our desires and goals. When we align the *Art of Visualization* with the principles of the law

of attraction, we can harness its full potential to attract abundance and opportunities into our lives. In this section, we will explore how visualization can be used as a manifestation tool and provide insights on enhancing our manifestation success through its practice.

A. Aligning Visualization with the Law of Attraction

The *Art of Visualization* and the law of attraction go hand in hand. Both concepts emphasize the power of thoughts, beliefs, and emotions in shaping our reality. Visualization allows us to create vivid mental images of our desires, engaging our senses and emotions to make them feel real and attainable. By aligning our visualizations with the principles of the law of attraction, we focus our energy and intention on attracting what we want into our lives. Through consistent practice, we train our minds to believe in the possibility of our desires manifesting, ultimately aligning our vibration with the frequency of what we wish to attract.

B. Enhancing Manifestation Success Through Visualization

Visualization acts as a catalyst for manifestation success by providing clarity, focus, and unwavering belief in our desired outcomes. When we visualize our goals with intensity and conviction, we send a clear message to the universe about what we want to attract. It helps us create a mental blueprint of our desires, making them more tangible and real. As we consistently visualize, our subconscious mind begins to accept these images as the truth, prompting us to take inspired action and seize opportunities that align with our visualized goals. Visualization amplifies our manifestation efforts by acting as a powerful magnet for the experiences, people, and circumstances that will bring our desires into reality.

C. Using Visualization to Attract Abundance and Opportunities

Visualization can be particularly effective in attracting abundance and opportunities into our lives. By vividly visualizing ourselves in a state of abundance, we shift our focus from lack to abundance, thereby attracting more prosperity into our experience. As we engage in the *Art of Visualization*, we imagine ourselves surrounded by abundance, success, and opportunities. We visualize the specific experiences, circumstances, and connections that align with our desires for abundance. By consistently practicing this form of visualization, we create a powerful energetic alignment with abundance and attract the resources and opportunities necessary to manifest our goals.

Summary

Visualization is a potent manifestation tool that allows us to align our energy, thoughts, and beliefs with the law of attraction. By embracing the *Art of Visualization*, we enhance our manifestation success, attract abundance and opportunities, and shape our reality according to our desires. Through visualization, we tap into the power of our subconscious mind, imprinting our goals and aspirations into our consciousness. As we consistently practice visualization with focus, belief, and gratitude, we become active participants in the co-creation of our lives. Embrace the *Art of Visualization* as a manifestation tool and open yourself to the infinite possibilities that await you. Visualize your dreams, believe in their manifestation, and watch as your reality effortlessly transforms to reflect your visualized desires.

Part 9: Advanced Techniques and Practices

As we continue our exploration of the *Art of Visualization*, it is important to delve into advanced techniques and practices that can further enhance our manifestation abilities. In this section, we will explore how visualization can be utilized for personal growth and self-improvement, the power of group visualization and collective intention setting, and the benefits of guided visualization and visualization aids. These advanced techniques offer new dimensions to the practice of visualization, allowing us to deepen our connection with our desires and manifest them with greater clarity and effectiveness.

A. Visualization for Personal Growth and Self-Improvement

Beyond manifesting external desires, visualization can be a transformative tool for personal growth and self-improvement. By visualizing our ideal self, we can tap into our unlimited potential and cultivate the qualities and characteristics we wish to embody. Through the *Art of Visualization*, we create a mental picture of our future self, engaging our emotions and senses to anchor this vision within our subconscious mind. As we consistently practice visualizing our desired personal growth, we align ourselves with the traits, behaviors, and experiences that support our development. Visualization becomes a powerful tool for self-motivation, self-belief, and self-empowerment, driving us towards the realization of our highest potential.

B. Group Visualization and Collective Intention Setting

The collective energy generated through group visualization and collective intention setting can exponentially amplify the manifestation process. When individuals come together with a shared vision and intention, their combined focus and energy create a powerful field of manifestation. Group visualization allows for the synchronization of thoughts, beliefs, and emotions, creating a harmonious resonance that attracts the desired outcomes more swiftly. By participating in group visualization sessions or engaging in collective intention setting exercises, we tap into the collective consciousness, accessing a vast reservoir of creative energy and support. This collective synergy strengthens our belief in the manifestation process and expands our capacity to create positive change not only in our lives but also in the world around us.

C. Exploring Guided Visualization and Visualization Aids

Guided visualization and visualization aids can be valuable tools for enhancing the depth and effectiveness of our visualization practice. Guided visualization involves following a recorded or live script that directs our imagination and takes us on a journey through the desired experience. This technique provides structure and guidance, making it easier to enter a focused and receptive state of mind. Visualization aids, such as vision boards, affirmations, and symbolic objects, serve as tangible reminders and reinforcement of our visualized desires. They act as visual cues that keep us aligned with our goals throughout the day. By incorporating guided visualization and visualization aids into our practice, we enhance our ability to immerse ourselves fully in the *Art of Visualization* and strengthen our connection with the desired manifestations.

Summary
In the realm of visualization, there are advanced techniques and practices that offer profound opportunities for personal growth, collective manifestation, and the refinement of our visualization skills. By utilizing visualization for personal growth and self-improvement, we harness its transformative potential to align ourselves with our highest aspirations. Engaging in group visualization and collective intention setting amplifies our manifestation efforts through the power of shared focus and intention. Exploring guided visualization and visualization aids provides structure, support, and reinforcement, deepening our connection with our visualized desires. As we embrace these advanced techniques and practices, we expand our capacity to create the reality we envision, and the *Art of Visualization* becomes a truly transformative and empowering tool in our lives. Embrace these advanced techniques, explore new possibilities, and witness the remarkable impact they can have on your manifestation journey.

Part 10: Case Studies and Success Stories

In our exploration of the *Art of Visualization*, it is inspiring and motivating to delve into real-life examples of individuals who have achieved their dreams through the power of visualization. By examining their success stories, we gain valuable insights into the common factors and strategies behind their accomplishments. These case studies provide us with inspiration, practical guidance, and a deeper understanding of how the *Art of Visualization* can be effectively applied to manifest our own desires. Let's explore these real-life examples and uncover the valuable lessons they offer.

A. Real-Life Examples of Individuals who Have Achieved Their Dreams Through Visualization

There are countless stories of individuals who have utilized the *Art of Visualization* to manifest their dreams and create remarkable transformations in their lives. From athletes to entrepreneurs, artists to scientists, people from all walks of life have harnessed the power of visualization to turn their aspirations into reality. These real-life examples serve as powerful evidence of the potential that lies within each of us to shape our destinies through focused intention and visualization. By examining these success stories, we gain a sense of possibility and inspiration that fuels our own manifestation journey.

B. Analyzing the Common Factors and Strategies Behind Their Success

When we analyze the success stories of those who have achieved their dreams through visualization, we can identify common factors and strategies that contribute to their success. While each person's journey is unique, there are often shared elements that contribute to their manifestation achievements. These factors may include unwavering belief in the power of visualization, consistent and dedicated practice, maintaining a positive mindset, aligning actions with intentions, and adapting their strategies as needed. By understanding and studying these common factors, we can incorporate them into our own visualization practice and increase our chances of success.

C. Drawing Inspiration and Lessons from Their Experiences

The success stories of individuals who have mastered the *Art of Visualization* offer valuable lessons and inspiration that we can apply to our own lives. By immersing ourselves in their experiences, we gain insights into the mindset, practices, and approaches that have propelled them towards their dreams. We can learn from their challenges, setbacks, and triumphs, adapting their strategies to suit our own aspirations. These stories remind us that we are not alone on our journey and that the *Art of Visualization* has the potential to create profound transformations in our lives. They ignite our belief in our own abilities and inspire us to persist in our visualization practice, knowing that we too can manifest our dreams.

Summary

Examining the case studies and success stories of individuals who have achieved their dreams through the *Art of Visualization* provides us with valuable insights, inspiration, and practical guidance. These real-life examples remind us of the limitless potential within us and the power of focused intention. By analyzing the common factors and strategies behind their success, we gain a deeper understanding of how to effectively apply visualization in our own lives. Drawing inspiration and lessons from their experiences, we infuse our own manifestation journey with renewed motivation and belief. The stories of these individuals serve as a testament to the transformative power of the *Art of Visualization* and inspire us to harness its potential to create our own success stories. Let their achievements guide and inspire you as you embrace the *Art of Visualization* and manifest your dreams into reality.

Conclusion: The Art of Visualization

In our exploration of the *Art of Visualization*, we have uncovered the transformative power it holds in painting our dreams into existence. Through understanding the definition, purpose, and techniques of visualization, we have discovered its connection to manifestation and the profound impact it has on our subconscious mind. We have explored various aspects, including the power of mental imagery, visualization for goal achievement, overcoming challenges, integrating visualization into daily life, and its influence on emotional well-being and manifestation. Now, let's recap the key insights and benefits of visualization, encourage continued practice, and discuss the next steps in our journey towards manifesting happiness through this powerful tool.

Throughout our exploration, we have gained valuable insights into the *Art of Visualization*. We have learned that visualization involves creating vivid mental images of our desired outcomes, incorporating sensory details, and harnessing the emotional impact of our visualizations. By setting clear intentions and goals, creating a conducive environment, and utilizing visualization techniques, we enhance our ability to manifest our dreams. We have also discovered that visualization helps in overcoming challenges such as skepticism, doubt, and limiting beliefs, while improving focus and concentration during practice. Visualization empowers us to cultivate positive emotions, heal and release emotional wounds, and visualize a happier and more fulfilling life. Furthermore, we have explored how visualization aligns with the law of attraction and serves as a powerful manifestation tool for attracting abundance and opportunities.

As we conclude our journey through the *Art of Visualization*, I encourage you to continue practicing and exploring this powerful technique. Visualization is a skill that can be developed and refined with consistent practice. Embrace the opportunity to visualize your dreams, goals, and desires regularly. Allow yourself to immerse in the vivid mental images, engage your senses, and harness the emotional impact of your visualizations. Remember that persistence, belief, and alignment of actions with intentions are key elements for manifestation success. By integrating visualization into your daily routines, meditation practices, and various aspects of your life, you amplify its effectiveness and create a deeper connection with your desired outcomes.

As you continue your journey towards manifesting happiness through visualization, there are a few important next steps to consider. First, reflect on your visualization practice and assess the areas where you can refine and enhance your techniques. Experiment with different approaches, such as guided visualizations and visualization aids, to explore new dimensions of the art. Seek inspiration from success stories and case studies, drawing lessons and strategies from those who have achieved their dreams through visualization. Additionally, surround yourself with a supportive environment and like-minded individuals who share your passion for manifestation and personal growth. Finally, remain open to the possibilities that visualization can bring into your life, nurturing your belief in its power to create profound transformations.

The *Art of Visualization* is a remarkable tool that empowers us to paint our dreams into existence. By recapitulating the key insights and benefits we have explored, we reaffirm the importance of visualization in manifesting our desires. Through visualization, we tap into the depths of our subconscious mind, align ourselves with the law of attraction, and unleash our creative potential. I encourage you to embrace the *Art of Visualization*, integrating it into your daily life, and exploring advanced techniques and practices. By nurturing your visualization skills and persistently aligning your intentions and actions, you embark on a transformative journey towards manifesting happiness, abundance, and fulfillment. Trust in the power of your visualization practice and unleash the creative forces within you to bring your dreams into vibrant reality.

Unlock the power of visualization and manifest your dreams with "The Art of Visualization: Painting Your Dreams into Existence," a comprehensive guide to harnessing the transformative potential of visualization techniques.

Chapter 4: Harnessing the Energy of Manifestation:
Aligning Your Thoughts and Emotions

Welcome to this article on "Harnessing the Energy of Manifestation: Aligning Your Thoughts and Emotions." In the exciting journey of manifesting your desires, understanding the crucial role of aligning your thoughts and emotions becomes paramount. By aligning these powerful forces within you, you can tap into the energetic flow that propels your manifestations into reality.

The power of manifestation lies not only in the thoughts we think but also in the emotions we feel. When our thoughts and emotions are in harmony and aligned with our desires, we become magnets for attracting what we truly want. However, if our thoughts and emotions are out of sync, sending mixed signals to the universe, we may experience challenges in manifesting our dreams.

Aligning our thoughts and emotions is essential because they generate the energetic frequency that interacts with the universe's vibrational field. When our thoughts and emotions are aligned with what we desire, we emit a strong and focused signal that resonates with corresponding opportunities and experiences.

In this article, we will explore various aspects of aligning your thoughts and emotions to harness the *Energy of Manifestation*. We will delve into the understanding of the power behind thoughts and emotions, how they influence our reality, and techniques to shift negative thought patterns.

Additionally, we will discuss the importance of cultivating positive emotions and how they act as catalysts for manifestation. You will discover practical strategies to align your thoughts and emotions with your desires, including visualization exercises, affirmations, and setting clear intentions.

Moreover, we will address the common challenges of resistance and doubt that can hinder alignment. You will learn how to overcome these obstacles and develop a mindset of belief and unwavering faith in the manifestation process.

Furthermore, we will explore how to maintain alignment in your daily life by integrating alignment practices into your routines and leveraging the power of intuition to guide your decisions.

By the end of this article, you will have gained valuable insights and practical tools to align your thoughts and emotions, allowing you to tap into the *Energy of Manifestation* and bring your desires into fruition.

So, let us embark on this transformative journey of aligning your thoughts and emotions to harness the *Energy of Manifestation* and create a life filled with abundance, joy, and fulfillment.

Part 1: Understanding the Power of Thoughts and Emotions

In this section, we will delve into the profound influence that thoughts and emotions have on the manifestation process. By understanding the role they play and recognizing their connection to energy, we can begin harnessing the *Energy of Manifestation* more effectively. Moreover, we will explore the impact of negative thoughts and emotions on our ability to manifest our desires.

A. Exploring the Role of Thoughts and Emotions in the Manifestation Process

Thoughts and emotions are powerful forces that shape our experiences and reality. Our thoughts are like seeds, planting the intentions for what we desire to manifest, while emotions infuse these thoughts with energy and vibrational frequency. Together, they create a magnetic force that attracts corresponding circumstances, people, and opportunities into our lives.

When our thoughts and emotions are aligned with our desires, we send a clear and focused signal to the universe. This alignment allows us to tap into the energetic flow of manifestation, increasing the likelihood of bringing our dreams to fruition. By understanding the power of thoughts and emotions, we gain the ability to consciously direct our manifestation process.

B. Recognizing the Connection Between Thoughts, Emotions, and Energy

Thoughts and emotions are not isolated entities but are intricately connected to the energy that permeates everything in the universe. Every thought we think and every emotion we feel carries its own vibrational frequency, which interacts with the energetic field around us. This field is responsive to our energetic output, attracting or repelling experiences based on the frequency we emit.

When our thoughts and emotions are aligned and emanate positive energy, we create a harmonious resonance with the universe. This alignment allows us to become co-creators of our reality, influencing the events and circumstances that come into our lives. By recognizing the connection between our thoughts, emotions, and the *Energy of Manifestation*, we gain the power to consciously shape our experiences.

C. Understanding the Impact of Negative Thoughts and Emotions on Manifestation

Negative thoughts and emotions can act as significant obstacles to manifesting our desires. When we harbor doubt, fear, or negativity, we emit a conflicting vibrational frequency that hinders the manifestation process. These negative energies create resistance, preventing the free flow of positive manifestations into our lives.

It is crucial to understand that the universe responds not only to our conscious desires but also to the underlying beliefs and emotions we hold within. If we consistently dwell in negative thoughts and emotions, we unintentionally attract unwanted experiences and hinder the manifestation of our true desires.

By recognizing the impact of negative thoughts and emotions, we can actively work on transforming them into positive and empowering ones. Through various techniques and practices, we can release limiting beliefs, cultivate optimism, and consciously choose thoughts and emotions that support our manifestation goals.

Summary
Understanding the power of thoughts and emotions is essential for harnessing the *Energy of Manifestation*. By exploring the role they play, recognizing their connection to energy, and understanding the impact of negativity, we can begin to consciously align our thoughts and emotions with our desires. As we continue our journey, let us delve deeper into practical techniques and strategies to enhance the harmony between our thoughts, emotions, and the *Energy of Manifestation*.

Part 2: Shifting Negative Thought Patterns

In this section, we will explore the transformative process of shifting negative thought patterns to align with the *Energy of Manifestation*. By identifying and reframing limiting beliefs, practicing positive self-talk, and utilizing affirmations, we can harness the power of our thoughts to manifest our desires more effectively.

A. Identifying Negative Thought Patterns and Limiting Beliefs

Negative thought patterns and limiting beliefs act as roadblocks on our path to manifestation. These patterns often stem from past experiences, societal conditioning, or self-doubt. It is crucial to identify and become aware of these patterns to begin the process of transforming them.

Take a moment to observe your thoughts and notice any recurring negative patterns. Pay attention to the beliefs that may be holding you back, such as "I'm not worthy," "I always fail," or "I don't deserve happiness." By recognizing these negative thought patterns and limiting beliefs, you can take the first step towards shifting them.

B. Techniques for Reframing Negative Thoughts into Positive Ones

Once you have identified negative thought patterns and limiting beliefs, the next step is to reframe them into positive and empowering thoughts. Reframing involves consciously replacing negative thoughts with positive alternatives.

One effective technique is to question the validity and accuracy of your negative thoughts. Challenge their truthfulness by asking yourself, "Is this thought serving me? Is there evidence to support a different perspective?" By questioning and challenging negative thoughts, you open the door to new possibilities and alternative viewpoints.

Additionally, focus on finding positive aspects and silver linings in challenging situations. Instead of dwelling on what went wrong, shift your attention to what you have learned or the opportunities that may arise from the experience. By reframing negative thoughts into positive ones, you harness the *Energy of Manifestation* and create a more supportive mindset.

C. Affirmations and Positive Self-Talk to Reprogram the Mind
Affirmations and positive self-talk are powerful tools for reprogramming the mind and aligning your thoughts with the *Energy of Manifestation*. Affirmations are positive statements that reinforce desired beliefs and outcomes.

Create a list of affirmations that counteract your negative thought patterns and limiting beliefs. For example, if you struggle with self-doubt, affirmations like "I am capable and deserving of success" or "I trust in my abilities to manifest my dreams" can be helpful. Repeat these affirmations regularly, preferably in front of a mirror, to reinforce positive beliefs and reprogram your subconscious mind.

Alongside affirmations, practice positive self-talk throughout your day. Be kind and compassionate to yourself, replacing self-criticism with supportive and encouraging words. Celebrate your successes, no matter how small, and acknowledge your progress. By incorporating affirmations and positive self-talk into your daily routine, you reinforce the alignment between your thoughts, emotions, and the *Energy of Manifestation*.

Summary
Shifting negative thought patterns is a vital step in harnessing the *Energy of Manifestation*. By identifying negative thought patterns and limiting beliefs, reframing negative thoughts into positive ones, and utilizing affirmations and positive self-talk, we can reprogram our minds for success. Remember, the

thoughts we cultivate shape our reality, so let us continue our journey with an empowered and positive mindset, ready to manifest our desires with aligned thoughts and emotions.

Part 3: Cultivating Positive Emotions

In this section, we will delve into the significance of cultivating positive emotions and how they play a pivotal role in harnessing the *Energy of Manifestation*. By recognizing their importance, practicing gratitude and joy, and utilizing emotion-based visualization, we can amplify the manifestation process and attract our desires with greater ease.

A. Recognizing the Importance of Positive Emotions in Manifestation

Positive emotions serve as powerful fuel for manifestation. When we experience feelings of joy, gratitude, love, and excitement, we elevate our vibrational frequency and align ourselves with the energy of what we desire. Positive emotions create a magnetic attraction that draws our manifestations closer to us.

By understanding the connection between emotions and manifestation, we realize that our emotional state acts as a powerful signal to the universe. When we cultivate positive emotions, we emit a frequency that resonates with abundance and possibility, thereby increasing the likelihood of manifesting our desires.

B. Practices for Cultivating Positive Emotions, such as Gratitude and Joy

Cultivating positive emotions requires conscious effort and practice. Two effective practices for nurturing positive emotions are gratitude and joy.

Gratitude is the practice of acknowledging and appreciating the blessings, abundance, and positive aspects of our lives. By regularly expressing gratitude for what we already have, we shift our focus from lack to abundance, fostering a sense of contentment and opening ourselves to receive more blessings.

Similarly, joy is a powerful emotion that propels manifestation. Engage in activities that bring you joy,

85

whether it's spending time in nature, pursuing hobbies, connecting with loved ones, or practicing self-care. Cultivating joy allows us to tap into our natural state of bliss and aligns us with the *Energy of Manifestation*.

C. Emotion-Based Visualization to Amplify the Manifestation Process

Visualization is a powerful tool in manifestation, and when combined with positive emotions, it becomes even more potent. Emotion-based visualization involves mentally and emotionally immersing ourselves in the experience of already having our desired manifestations.

When practicing visualization, engage all your senses to make it more vivid and real. Feel the emotions associated with achieving your desires, whether it's the excitement, joy, or gratitude. Immerse yourself in the details of your vision, creating a clear and vibrant mental image of your desired outcome.

As you visualize, allow the positive emotions to flow through you, knowing that you are already in possession of what you desire. By infusing your visualizations with strong positive emotions, you are harnessing the *Energy of Manifestation* and signaling to the universe that you are aligned and ready to receive.

Summary

Cultivating positive emotions is an essential aspect of harnessing the *Energy of Manifestation*. Through the practices of gratitude and joy, we elevate our vibrational frequency and create a magnetic attraction for our desires. By combining positive emotions with visualization, we amplify the manifestation process, signaling our readiness to receive what we seek. Embrace the power of positive emotions, nurture them daily, and infuse them into your visualization practice. As you continue this journey of aligning your thoughts and emotions, remember that your positive emotions are a powerful catalyst for manifesting the life of your dreams.

Part 4: Aligning Thoughts and Emotions with Desires
In this section, we will explore powerful techniques to align our thoughts and emotions with our desires, enabling us to harness the *Energy of Manifestation*. By setting clear intentions and goals, engaging in visualization exercises, and utilizing affirmations and positive visualization, we can enhance our alignment and accelerate the manifestation process.

A. Setting Clear Intentions and Goals to Focus Thoughts and Emotions
Setting clear intentions and goals is a crucial step in aligning our thoughts and emotions with our desires. When we have a clear vision of what we want to manifest, it provides a focal point for our thoughts and emotions.

Take the time to define your intentions and goals with clarity. Write them down and revisit them regularly to keep them fresh in your mind. As you do so, allow yourself to feel the excitement and anticipation that comes with the realization of your desires. By aligning your thoughts and emotions with your intentions, you create a powerful energy that propels you towards manifestation.

B. Visualization Exercises for Aligning Thoughts and Emotions with Desires
Visualization is a potent tool for aligning our thoughts and emotions with our desires. Engaging in visualization exercises helps us create a detailed mental image of our desired outcomes, allowing us to immerse ourselves in the experience of already having what we seek.

Find a quiet and comfortable space where you can relax. Close your eyes and visualize your desired manifestation with vivid detail. Imagine yourself living that reality, feeling the emotions associated with it. As you visualize, let go of any doubts or limitations and fully embrace the belief that your desires are already on their way to you. This practice aligns your thoughts and emotions with the *Energy of Manifestation*, reinforcing your intention and attracting your desires towards you.

C. Using Affirmations and Positive Visualization to Reinforce Alignment

Affirmations and positive visualization are powerful tools for reinforcing the alignment of our thoughts and emotions with our desires. By incorporating these practices into our daily routine, we can continuously program our minds for success and maintain a positive focus.

Choose affirmations that resonate with your desires and repeat them regularly. Affirmations are positive statements that affirm the reality of your desires. For example, if your desire is to attract abundance, you can repeat affirmations such as "I am a magnet for abundance" or "I attract unlimited prosperity into my life." Combine these affirmations with positive visualization, where you mentally see yourself already living the abundant life you desire. This combination strengthens your alignment and helps you overcome any doubts or negative thoughts that may arise.

Summary

Aligning our thoughts and emotions with our desires is a fundamental aspect of harnessing the *Energy of Manifestation*. By setting clear intentions and goals, engaging in visualization exercises, and utilizing affirmations and positive visualization, we reinforce our alignment and accelerate the manifestation process. Remember, clarity, focus, and belief are key to aligning your thoughts and emotions with your desires. Embrace these practices and continue to cultivate alignment as you move forward on your journey of manifestation. Harness the *Energy of Manifestation* and watch as your desires manifest into reality.

Part 5: Overcoming Resistance and Doubt

In this section, we will delve into the importance of overcoming resistance and doubt in harnessing the *Energy of Manifestation*. Addressing these obstacles is essential for maintaining alignment and allowing our desires to manifest effortlessly. By recognizing and addressing resistance and self-doubt, utilizing techniques for releasing resistance, and cultivating a mindset of unwavering faith, we can overcome these challenges and accelerate our manifestation journey.

A. Addressing Resistance and Self-Doubt That Hinder Alignment

Resistance and self-doubt are common hurdles that can hinder our alignment with our desires. They often arise from past experiences, limiting beliefs, or fear of the unknown. It's crucial to address these obstacles to create a clear pathway for manifestation.

Start by identifying any resistance or self-doubt that arises within you. Pay attention to the thoughts and emotions that surface when you think about your desires. Are there any doubts or fears holding you back? By acknowledging these obstacles, you gain awareness and can begin to work through them.

B. Techniques for Releasing Resistance and Embracing Trust

Releasing resistance is a key step in overcoming doubt and allowing alignment to flow. Several techniques can help in this process, such as:

1. Awareness and Acceptance: Become aware of your resistance and accept it without judgment. Acknowledge that it is a normal part of the manifestation journey. By accepting resistance, you create space for transformation.
2. Emotional Release: Allow yourself to express and release any negative emotions associated with resistance. This could be through journaling, talking with a trusted friend, or engaging in activities that help you process emotions, such as meditation or exercise.
3. Affirmations and Positive Reinforcement: Utilize affirmations that counteract resistance and self-doubt. Repeat positive statements that affirm your belief in the manifestation process and your ability to achieve your desires.

C. Cultivating a Mindset of Belief and Unwavering Faith in Manifestation

Cultivating a mindset of belief and unwavering faith is vital for maintaining alignment and overcoming resistance and doubt. Trusting in the process of manifestation creates a powerful energy that supports the realization of our desires.

Develop a daily practice of reinforcing your belief in manifestation. Engage in activities that boost your confidence, such as visualization exercises, gratitude practice, or affirmations. Surround yourself with positive influences, whether it be through reading inspiring books, listening to motivational audios, or connecting with like-minded individuals.

Remember that belief and unwavering faith are choices. Choose to believe in the power of manifestation and in your ability to align with your desires. Trust that the universe is supporting you and that everything is working in your favor.

Summary
Overcoming resistance and doubt is a crucial step in harnessing the *Energy of Manifestation*. By addressing resistance and self-doubt, utilizing techniques for releasing resistance, and cultivating a mindset of unwavering faith, we create a powerful alignment that propels us towards our desires. Trust in the process, believe in yourself, and continue to nurture your alignment as you move forward on your manifestation journey. Harness the *Energy of Manifestation* and watch as your desires become your reality.

Part 6: Maintaining Alignment in Daily Life
In this section, we will explore the importance of maintaining alignment in our daily lives to harness the *Energy of Manifestation* consistently. Integrating alignment practices into our routines and habits, cultivating mindfulness and awareness, and making necessary adjustments to our thoughts and emotions are essential for staying aligned throughout the day. By prioritizing alignment in our daily lives, we create a solid foundation for the manifestation of our desires.

A. Integrating Alignment Practices into Daily Routines and Habits
To maintain alignment, it is helpful to incorporate alignment practices into our daily routines and habits. This creates a consistent and supportive environment for the manifestation process.

Start by setting aside dedicated time each day for alignment practices. This could be in the morning, before bed, or during breaks throughout the day. Engage in activities such as meditation, visualization, affirmations, or journaling to connect with your desires and reinforce alignment.

Additionally, find ways to infuse alignment into your daily tasks. Practice gratitude while doing chores or use positive affirmations during your commute. By consciously infusing alignment into your routines and habits, you create a continuous flow of energy that supports your manifestation journey.

B. Mindfulness and Awareness to Stay Aligned Throughout the Day

Mindfulness and awareness play a vital role in maintaining alignment throughout the day. Cultivating present-moment awareness allows us to observe our thoughts, emotions, and actions, and make conscious choices that support alignment.

Practice mindfulness by regularly checking in with yourself. Notice your thoughts and emotions without judgment. If you sense any resistance or negativity creeping in, take a moment to realign your focus and choose thoughts that support your desires.

Furthermore, pay attention to the external influences and environments that affect your alignment. Surround yourself with positive and uplifting people, engage in activities that bring you joy, and minimize exposure to negativity or situations that drain your energy. By staying mindful of your surroundings and consciously making choices that support alignment, you create a conducive environment for manifestation.

C. Adjusting Thoughts and Emotions as Needed to Maintain Alignment

Maintaining alignment requires us to be flexible and willing to adjust our thoughts and emotions as needed. We are human, and it's natural for occasional challenges or distractions to arise. The key is to be proactive in managing them.

Regularly check in with your thoughts and emotions throughout the day. If you notice any negativity or thoughts that deviate from alignment, consciously choose to shift them towards positive and supportive ones. Practice reframing negative situations and choosing empowering perspectives.

Emotions also play a crucial role in maintaining alignment. If you find yourself experiencing negative emotions, take time to process and release them. Engage in activities that uplift your spirits, such as physical exercise, listening to music, or spending time in nature. By actively managing your thoughts and emotions, you keep the *Energy of Manifestation* flowing and maintain alignment.

Summary
Maintaining alignment in our daily lives is fundamental to harnessing the *Energy of Manifestation* consistently. By integrating alignment practices into our routines, cultivating mindfulness and awareness, and making necessary adjustments to our thoughts and emotions, we create a harmonious environment that supports our manifestation journey. Stay present, be mindful of your thoughts and emotions, and make conscious choices that align with your desires. Harness the *Energy of Manifestation* and watch as your dreams unfold in your daily life.

Part 7: Harnessing the Power of Intuition
In the journey of aligning our thoughts and emotions to harness the *Energy of Manifestation*, the power of intuition serves as a valuable guide. Intuition, often referred to as our inner knowing or gut feeling, has the ability to provide us with insights and guidance that support our alignment and manifestation process. In this section, we will explore the role of intuition, techniques for connecting with and trusting it, and how to use intuition to make aligned decisions and take inspired action.

A. Recognizing the Role of Intuition in Guiding Alignment
Intuition is a natural and inherent aspect of our being that can serve as a compass in our manifestation journey. It is that inner voice or feeling that nudges us towards what feels right

and aligned with our desires. Recognizing the role of intuition in guiding alignment is key to utilizing its power effectively.

Pay attention to the subtle messages and sensations that arise within you. Notice when something resonates deeply or when a decision feels aligned without logical explanation. Intuition often communicates through feelings, hunches, or a sense of knowing. By acknowledging and honoring these intuitive signals, we can navigate our alignment journey with greater clarity and ease.

B. Techniques for Connecting with and Trusting Intuition
Connecting with and trusting our intuition requires cultivating a deeper sense of self-awareness and openness. Here are some techniques to help you strengthen your connection with your intuition:

1. Quiet the mind: Find moments of stillness through meditation, deep breathing, or contemplation. By quieting the mind, you create space for intuitive insights to surface.
2. Listen to your body: Our bodies often provide subtle signals that indicate whether something is aligned or not. Pay attention to sensations, such as a lightness or heaviness in your chest or a feeling of expansion or contraction in your body.
3. Journaling: Engage in reflective journaling to tap into your intuition. Write down questions or concerns and allow your intuition to guide your writing. Notice any intuitive insights that arise.

Trust your initial impressions: When faced with decisions or choices, trust your initial impressions. Often, the first instinct is aligned with your intuition before doubts or fears cloud your judgment.

C. Using Intuition to Make Aligned Decisions and Take Inspired Action
Intuition can be a powerful tool for making aligned decisions and taking inspired action in the manifestation process. When you align your thoughts and emotions, and then listen

to your intuition, you enhance your ability to make choices that are in harmony with your desires.

When faced with decisions, pause and tune in to your intuition. Ask yourself what feels right and in alignment with your desires. Trust the guidance that comes forth and let it inform your choices.

Furthermore, use your intuition to identify inspired actions that move you closer to your desired manifestations. Intuition can provide insights on steps to take, opportunities to explore, or connections to make. By following these intuitive nudges, you tap into the flow of manifestation energy and take actions that are in perfect alignment with your desires.

Summary
Harnessing the power of intuition is an integral part of aligning our thoughts and emotions to harness the *Energy of Manifestation*. By recognizing the role of intuition in guiding alignment, practicing techniques to connect with and trust our intuition, and using it to make aligned decisions and take inspired action, we align ourselves with the highest possibilities for manifestation. Trust your intuition as a guiding force on your journey and watch as the *Energy of Manifestation* supports the realization of your desires.

Part 8: The Ripple Effect of Alignment
As we delve deeper into the practice of aligning our thoughts and emotions to harness the *Energy of Manifestation*, it becomes evident that alignment has a profound impact that extends beyond the realm of our desires. In this section, we will explore the ripple effect of alignment, understanding how it positively impacts other areas of life, spreads positive energy and attracts synchronicities, and ultimately cultivates a life of alignment, joy, and fulfillment.

A. Understanding How Alignment Positively Impacts Other Areas of Life
Alignment is not limited to the manifestation of specific desires; it permeates every aspect of our existence. When we align our thoughts and emotions, we create a harmonious

energetic resonance that affects all areas of our lives. Here are a few ways alignment positively impacts other areas of life:

1. Relationships: When we are in alignment, our relationships naturally flourish. We emanate positive energy, which attracts harmonious connections and deepens existing bonds.
2. Health and Well-being: Alignment promotes a state of balance and well-being within our physical, mental, and emotional selves. It supports optimal health and vitality, allowing us to thrive in all aspects of life.
3. Career and Abundance: Alignment opens doors to opportunities and abundance. By aligning our thoughts and emotions with success and prosperity, we attract the resources, connections, and circumstances that support our professional growth and financial well-being.

B. Spreading Positive Energy and Attracting Synchronicities Through Alignment

When we harness the *Energy of Manifestation* through alignment, we become powerful magnets for positive energy and synchronicities. Alignment creates a ripple effect that extends into the world around us, influencing the experiences and interactions we attract. Here's how alignment contributes to this process:

1. Positive Energy: Alignment generates a vibrational frequency of positivity and joy. As we radiate this energy, we naturally uplift others and contribute to a positive and harmonious collective consciousness.
2. Synchronicities: Alignment aligns us with the flow of life, allowing synchronicities to unfold. Synchronicities are meaningful coincidences and serendipitous events that occur when we are in the right place at the right time, guided by the universe towards our desires.

By maintaining alignment and fostering positive energy, we create an environment that invites synchronicities and aligns us with the abundant possibilities of the universe.

C. Cultivating a Life of Alignment, Joy, and Fulfillment
Ultimately, the practice of alignment is about cultivating a life that is filled with joy, fulfillment, and purpose. It is a continuous journey of self-discovery, growth, and conscious creation. Here are some key aspects to consider on this path:

1. Self-Awareness: Develop a deep understanding of yourself, your desires, and your authentic values. Align your thoughts and emotions with what truly brings you joy and fulfillment.
2. Gratitude and Appreciation: Cultivate a mindset of gratitude and appreciation for the blessings in your life. By focusing on what you are grateful for, you amplify positive energy and attract more to be grateful for.
3. Consistency and Persistence: Alignment is a practice that requires consistent effort and persistence. Stay committed to aligning your thoughts and emotions with your desires, even during challenging times.

Summary
The ripple effect of alignment goes far beyond the manifestation of specific desires. It positively impacts all areas of our lives, spreading positive energy, attracting synchronicities, and creating a life of alignment, joy, and fulfillment. As we continue harnessing the *Energy of Manifestation* through alignment, we contribute to a more harmonious and abundant world, both for ourselves and those around us. Embrace the journey of alignment and witness the profound transformations that unfold in every aspect of your life.

Conclusion: Aligning Your Thoughts and Emotions
Aligning your thoughts and emotions is a powerful practice that allows you to harness the *Energy of Manifestation* and create the life you desire. Throughout this journey, we have delved into various aspects of alignment and discovered the immense potential it holds. Let's recap our key insights and takeaways:

Throughout this article, we have explored the importance of aligning our thoughts and emotions in the manifestation process. By recognizing the connection between our thoughts, emotions, and energy, we gain a deeper understanding of how they shape our reality. We have learned that negative thoughts and emotions can act as barriers to manifestation, but through techniques like reframing negative thoughts and using affirmations, we can shift our mindset and pave the way for positive outcomes.

Cultivating positive emotions has emerged as a vital aspect of alignment. By practicing gratitude, joy, and other positive emotions, we elevate our vibration and attract aligned experiences. Emotion-based visualization further amplifies the manifestation process, allowing us to tap into the power of our emotions to paint a vivid picture of our desired reality.

Aligning our thoughts and emotions with our desires is essential for manifestation success. Setting clear intentions and goals helps focus our energy and directs our actions towards their fulfillment. Visualization exercises and affirmations serve as powerful tools to reinforce alignment and strengthen our belief in the manifestation process.

Throughout this journey, we have also addressed the challenges that can arise, such as resistance and self-doubt. By acknowledging and releasing resistance, embracing trust, and cultivating a mindset of unwavering faith, we can overcome these obstacles and stay aligned on our path to manifestation.

As we conclude this article, I encourage you to continue practicing and exploring the art of aligning your thoughts and emotions. Consistency and perseverance are key on this journey. Embrace alignment as a daily practice, integrating it into your routines and habits. Stay mindful and aware, adjusting your thoughts and emotions as needed to maintain alignment throughout the day.

Remember, harnessing the *Energy of Manifestation* is a lifelong journey. It requires patience, dedication, and self-awareness. Embrace your intuition as a guiding force and trust in the process. As you align your thoughts and emotions, you will begin to witness the ripple effect it has on other areas of your life. Positive energy will radiate from within you, attracting synchronicities and opportunities that align with your desires.

So, take the next steps with confidence and enthusiasm. Embrace alignment as a way of life and watch as your thoughts and emotions collaborate to bring your dreams into existence. The power is within you, and the universe is ready to support your journey of manifestation. Embrace the art of aligning your thoughts and emotions, and manifest a life filled with joy, abundance, and fulfillment.

Chapter 5: Setting Clear Intentions: Navigating Your Path to Success

Welcome to "Setting Clear Intentions: Navigating Your Path to Success!" In this chapter, we will explore the significance of aligning your thoughts and emotions as you embark on a journey toward achieving your goals. *Setting Clear Intentions* is a powerful tool that can help you navigate your path to success with focus, purpose, and clarity.

When it comes to manifesting your desires, aligning your thoughts and emotions plays a crucial role. Your thoughts are like the seeds you plant, and your emotions are the nourishing soil in which those seeds grow. By aligning these two aspects, you harness the energy of manifestation and set in motion a powerful force that can bring your dreams into reality.

In this chapter, we will delve into the key aspects of *Setting Clear Intentions* and navigating your path to success. We will start by understanding the power of intentions and their connection to your thoughts and actions. Clarifying your desires and goals will be the next step, as we explore techniques to identify and define what you truly want to achieve.

We will then dive into the process of writing and affirming your intentions, exploring the importance of positive language and present tense in creating powerful statements. Strengthening your belief and alignment will be another focus, as we discuss strategies to cultivate unwavering faith in the realization of your intentions.

Taking inspired action is a vital component of success, and we will explore ways to proactively move forward on your path. Maintaining focus and resilience will also be addressed, as we offer guidance on staying committed and motivated despite challenges and distractions.

Throughout the chapter, we will emphasize the importance of regularly reviewing and revising your intentions, as your aspirations may evolve and change over time. By continuously aligning your intentions with your evolving desires, you ensure that your path remains in harmony with your truest ambitions.

So, are you ready to embark on this journey of *Setting Clear Intentions* and navigating your path to success? Let's dive in and discover the transformative power of aligning your thoughts and emotions to manifest the life you desire.

Part 1: Understanding the Power of Intentions
In this section, we will explore the immense power of intentions and their role in helping us achieve our goals. *Setting Clear Intentions* is like mapping out our desired destination on the journey to success. Let's delve into the significance of intentions and how they shape our thoughts and actions.

A. Definition and Significance of Intentions in Goal Attainment
Intentions can be defined as the conscious and deliberate thoughts and desires we hold regarding a specific outcome or goal. They serve as the compass that guides our actions and directs our focus towards what we truly want to achieve. *Setting Clear Intentions* helps us establish a strong foundation for our aspirations, providing us with a clear direction and purpose.

Intentions have a significant impact on our mindset and motivation. When we set intentions, we are essentially declaring our commitment to the desired outcome and aligning ourselves with the path that leads us there. They provide us with a sense of clarity and help us prioritize our actions, making it easier to make decisions that support our goals.

B. Recognizing the Role of Intentions in Shaping Thoughts and Actions
Our thoughts and actions are intricately linked to our intentions. When we set clear intentions, we begin to notice a shift in our thoughts and mindset. We become more aware of opportunities, possibilities, and solutions that align with our intentions. Our thoughts become aligned with our desires,

creating a positive and proactive mindset that fuels our actions.

Intentions shape our actions by influencing the choices we make and the steps we take towards our goals. When our intentions are clear, we naturally gravitate towards actions that support them. We become more focused, driven, and committed to taking the necessary steps to manifest our intentions into reality.

C. The Connection Between Intentions and Manifestation
Setting Clear Intentions is an essential step in the manifestation process. Intentions act as a powerful force that aligns our thoughts, emotions, and actions with the desired outcome. They send a clear message to the universe, signaling our commitment and readiness to receive what we seek.

By *Setting Clear Intentions*, we tap into the energy of manifestation and create a harmonious flow between our desires and the external world. Intentions serve as a bridge that connects our inner world with the outer world, allowing us to attract the resources, opportunities, and synchronicities that support our goals.

Summary
Understanding the power of intentions is fundamental to setting clear goals and achieving success. By recognizing the significance of intentions in goal attainment, understanding their influence on our thoughts and actions, and acknowledging their connection to manifestation, we lay the groundwork for navigating our path to success. *Setting Clear Intentions* becomes the compass that guides us as we embark on the journey towards realizing our aspirations. In the next sections, we will delve deeper into practical techniques and strategies for *Setting Clear Intentions* and aligning our thoughts and actions with our desired outcomes.

Part 2: Clarifying Your Desires and Goals
To effectively navigate your path to success, it is crucial to clarify your desires and set specific goals that align with your intentions. In this section, we will explore practical strategies

for gaining clarity, setting measurable goals, and creating visual representations of your aspirations.

A. Reflecting on Personal Desires and Aspirations
Setting Clear Intentions begins with understanding your personal desires and aspirations. Take the time to reflect on what truly matters to you and what you want to achieve in various areas of your life. Consider your career, relationships, health, personal growth, and any other aspects that hold significance for you.

Reflecting on your desires involves connecting with your authentic self and listening to the whispers of your heart. What brings you joy? What sparks your passion? What do you envision for your future? By exploring these questions, you can gain a deeper understanding of what you truly want to manifest in your life.

B. Setting Specific and Measurable Goals Aligned with Your Intentions
Once you have a clearer sense of your desires, it's time to set specific and measurable goals that align with your intentions. Specific goals provide clarity and direction, while measurable goals allow you to track your progress and celebrate your achievements along the way.

To set specific goals, break down your aspirations into actionable steps. Define the who, what, when, where, and how of your goals. Be as detailed as possible, outlining the specific actions you need to take and the resources you may require. This level of clarity enables you to focus your energy and efforts effectively.

Additionally, ensure that your goals are measurable. Set criteria that will allow you to evaluate your progress and determine whether you have successfully achieved your desired outcomes. Measurable goals provide a tangible framework for tracking your growth and staying motivated.

C. Creating a Vision Board or Visual Representation of Your Goals
Creating a vision board or visual representation of your goals is a powerful way to enhance the clarity and focus of your

intentions. A vision board is a collection of images, quotes, and symbols that represent your desires and goals. It serves as a visual reminder and reinforcement of your intentions.

To create a vision board, gather magazines, printouts, or digital images that resonate with your aspirations. Arrange them on a board or create a digital collage. Display your vision board in a prominent place where you will see it regularly. Allow it to inspire and motivate you as you work towards your goals.

The act of creating a vision board helps to solidify your intentions in your mind and aligns your subconscious with your conscious desires. It serves as a visual cue that continually reminds you of your aspirations and keeps you focused on manifesting them.

Summary

Clarifying your desires and setting specific, measurable goals that align with your intentions are essential steps in *Setting Clear Intentions*. By reflecting on your personal desires, setting specific goals, and creating a vision board or visual representation, you establish a clear roadmap for manifesting your aspirations. These practices enhance your clarity, focus, and commitment to the path of success. In the next sections, we will explore additional techniques and strategies to further align your thoughts and actions with your intentions, guiding you closer to the realization of your goals.

Part 3: Writing and Affirming Your Intentions

Setting Clear Intentions involves more than just having a general idea of what you want to achieve. It requires crafting clear and concise statements of intention, harnessing the power of positive language and present tense, and regularly affirming and revisiting your intentions. In this section, we will explore the significance of writing and affirming your intentions as powerful tools for manifestation.

A. Crafting Clear and Concise Statements of Intention

When setting intentions, it is important to articulate them in clear and concise statements. This clarity allows your mind to focus on the specific outcomes you desire to manifest. Take the time to think deeply about what you want to attract into your life and express it in a way that is both meaningful and straightforward.

Crafting clear statements of intention involves being specific about what you want to achieve or experience. Avoid vague or ambiguous language. Instead, use precise and descriptive words that capture the essence of your desires. By expressing your intentions with clarity, you provide a clear direction for your thoughts and actions.

B. The Power of Positive Language and Present Tense
The language you use when setting intentions plays a significant role in their manifestation. Positive language is crucial for aligning your energy with the desired outcomes. Instead of focusing on what you don't want, frame your intentions in a positive light. Emphasize what you do want to attract or create in your life.

Additionally, using the present tense in your statements of intention reinforces their power and immediacy. Rather than saying, "I will be successful," rephrase it as "I am successful." This shifts your mindset from a future-oriented mindset to a present-focused mindset. By affirming your intentions in the present tense, you align your thoughts and emotions with the energy of manifestation.

C. Regularly Affirming and Revisiting Your Intentions for Reinforcement
Affirmations are a powerful way to reinforce your intentions and reprogram your subconscious mind. By repeating positive statements aligned with your intentions, you establish a consistent and empowering mental dialogue. Affirmations help to counteract any negative or limiting beliefs that may arise and strengthen your alignment with your desired outcomes.

Make it a habit to regularly affirm your intentions. Choose a time and place where you can be in a calm and focused state. Repeat your affirmations with conviction and belief. Visualize yourself already living your intentions, feeling the emotions associated with their fulfillment. The more you reinforce your intentions through affirmations, the more you strengthen your energetic alignment with them.

In addition to affirmations, regularly revisiting your written statements of intention provides reinforcement and keeps them at the forefront of your consciousness. Review your intentions daily or as often as needed to remind yourself of your goals and stay connected to the energy of manifestation.

Summary
Writing and affirming your intentions are powerful practices that support the process of *Setting Clear Intentions*. By crafting clear and concise statements, using positive language and the present tense, and regularly affirming and revisiting your intentions, you strengthen your focus, align your energy, and enhance the manifestation process. In the next sections, we will delve deeper into techniques and strategies to further empower your journey of navigating the path to success through *Setting Clear Intentions*.

Part 4: Strengthening Your Belief and Alignment

Setting Clear Intentions is not enough on its own; it is equally important to strengthen your belief and alignment with those intentions. In this section, we will explore how to cultivate belief and faith in the realization of your intentions, overcome doubt and limiting beliefs through mindset shifts, and align your thoughts, emotions, and actions with your intentions.

A. Cultivating Belief and Faith in the Realization of Your Intentions

Belief and faith are powerful catalysts for manifestation. When you deeply believe in the possibility of your intentions becoming a reality, you create a fertile ground for their manifestation. Cultivating belief and faith involves developing a strong sense of trust in the universe and in your own abilities to create the outcomes you desire.

To strengthen your belief and faith, engage in practices that reinforce positive expectations and reinforce your connection to the energy of manifestation. Surround yourself with supportive and like-minded individuals who inspire and uplift you. Seek out success stories and examples of people who have achieved similar goals, as this can further enhance your belief in what is possible.

Remember to celebrate even the smallest signs of progress or alignment with your intentions. Each small step forward reaffirms your belief and generates positive momentum towards the realization of your goals.

B. Overcoming Doubt and Limiting Beliefs Through Mindset Shifts

Doubt and limiting beliefs can hinder your progress and alignment with your intentions. It is important to identify and challenge these negative thought patterns to create space for new possibilities. Mindset shifts are essential for transforming doubt into belief and limiting beliefs into empowering beliefs.

Start by becoming aware of your self-talk and the thoughts that arise when you think about your intentions. Notice any doubts or limiting beliefs that surface and question their validity. Are these beliefs based on past experiences or societal conditioning? Challenge them by seeking evidence to the contrary and reframing them in a more positive and empowering light.

Replace limiting beliefs with affirmations and positive statements that support your intentions. Affirm your capabilities, worthiness, and the possibility of achieving your goals. As you consistently reinforce these positive beliefs, you rewire your mindset and align your thoughts with the energy of manifestation.

C. Aligning Thoughts, Emotions, and Actions with Your Intentions

Alignment is a crucial element in manifesting your intentions. It involves aligning your thoughts, emotions, and actions with the desired outcomes. When your thoughts, emotions, and actions are in harmony with your intentions, you create a powerful synergy that propels you towards success.

Pay attention to the thoughts that arise in your mind. Are they aligned with your intentions, or do they contradict them? Practice replacing negative or conflicting thoughts with positive, supportive thoughts that reinforce your belief and alignment.

Emotions also play a vital role in alignment. Cultivate positive emotions such as gratitude, joy, and excitement to strengthen your energetic connection with your intentions. Visualize yourself already experiencing the fulfillment of your goals and immerse yourself in the positive emotions associated with it.

Lastly, take inspired action aligned with your intentions. Break down your goals into actionable steps and consistently take small, intentional actions that move you closer to their realization. Each action you take reinforces your belief, aligns your energy, and brings you one step closer to the manifestation of your intentions.

Summary
Strengthening your belief and alignment is essential for successfully manifesting your intentions. By cultivating belief and faith, overcoming doubt and limiting beliefs through mindset shifts, and aligning your thoughts, emotions, and actions with your intentions, you empower yourself to navigate the path to success. In the upcoming sections, we will explore additional strategies and techniques to further enhance your ability to manifest your desires through *Setting Clear Intentions*.

Part 5: Taking Inspired Action
Setting Clear Intentions is the first step towards manifesting your desires, but it is through taking inspired action that you bring those intentions to life. In this section, we will explore the importance of proactive steps towards your intentions, how to identify actionable tasks and milestones on your path to success, and the significance of embracing opportunities and acting on intuition.

A. The Importance of Proactive Steps Towards Your Intentions
Intentions alone are not enough to manifest your desires. Taking proactive steps towards your intentions is vital for translating them into tangible results. When you take action,

you demonstrate your commitment and readiness to bring your intentions into reality.

Proactive steps involve actively seeking opportunities, acquiring the necessary skills and knowledge, and making conscious choices aligned with your intentions. It requires stepping out of your comfort zone and embracing growth and change. By taking initiative and responsibility for your own success, you harness the energy of manifestation and create momentum towards achieving your goals.

B. Identifying Actionable Tasks and Milestones on Your Path to Success

To effectively take inspired action, it is essential to break down your intentions into actionable tasks and milestones. Start by clarifying the specific actions you need to take to move closer to your desired outcome. Break down your goals into smaller, manageable steps that you can take consistently.

Identify milestones along the way that serve as indicators of progress and achievement. These milestones can provide you with a sense of accomplishment and motivation as you navigate your path to success. Celebrate each milestone reached, as it reinforces your belief and confidence in your ability to manifest your intentions.

Regularly reassess and adjust your action plan as needed. Stay flexible and open to new possibilities, as your journey may unfold in unexpected ways. Adaptability allows you to seize opportunities that align with your intentions and adjust your actions accordingly.

C. Embracing Opportunities and Acting on Intuition

Manifestation often presents opportunities that align with your intentions. Embracing these opportunities requires being open-minded and receptive to new experiences. Pay attention to synchronicities, signs, and intuitive nudges that guide you towards the right path.

Acting on your intuition is a powerful way to take inspired action. Trusting your inner guidance allows you to make decisions and take steps that align with your true desires. Tune in to your intuition by practicing mindfulness and cultivating self-awareness. Quiet your mind, listen to your inner voice, and trust the wisdom that arises from within.

Embrace the courage to step out of your comfort zone and take calculated risks. Be willing to explore new possibilities, even if they seem uncertain or unfamiliar. By embracing opportunities and acting on intuition, you align yourself with the flow of manifestation and create pathways for your intentions to manifest.

Summary
Taking inspired action is a key component of manifesting your intentions. By taking proactive steps towards your intentions, identifying actionable tasks and milestones, and embracing opportunities while acting on intuition, you set the stage for success. Remember that action is the bridge that connects your intentions to their physical manifestation. In the next section, we will delve deeper into the power of visualization and how it enhances the manifestation process through *Setting Clear Intentions*.

Part 6: Maintaining Focus and Resilience

Setting Clear Intentions and taking inspired action is a powerful combination, but the journey towards manifesting your desires is not always smooth sailing. In this section, we will explore strategies for maintaining focus amidst distractions and challenges, building resilience in the face of setbacks, and practicing self-care to nurture your motivation throughout the manifestation journey.

A. Strategies for Staying Focused Amidst Distractions and Challenges

Maintaining focus is crucial to staying on track with your intentions. In a world filled with distractions, it's important to establish strategies that help you stay centered and focused on what truly matters. Here are a few strategies to consider:

1. Prioritize and Simplify: Identify your key priorities and focus your energy on them. Simplify your tasks, eliminating unnecessary distractions and commitments that do not align with your intentions.

2. Create a Supportive Environment: Designate a dedicated space for your manifestation practice that promotes focus and minimizes distractions. Clear clutter, surround yourself with inspiring objects, and create a peaceful atmosphere conducive to concentration.
3. Time Management: Implement effective time management techniques, such as creating schedules, setting deadlines, and breaking tasks into manageable chunks. This helps you allocate time efficiently and avoid becoming overwhelmed by the demands of daily life.

B. Building Resilience and Perseverance in the Face of Setbacks

The manifestation journey is not always a smooth path, and setbacks or challenges may arise along the way. Building resilience is essential to navigate these obstacles and continue moving forward:

1. Re-frame Setbacks as Opportunities: View setbacks as opportunities for growth and learning. Embrace the lessons they offer and find ways to pivot and adjust your approach. Remember that setbacks do not define your ultimate success but are part of the journey.
2. Cultivate a Growth Mindset: Adopt a growth mindset that sees challenges as stepping stones to success. Embrace a belief that with effort, persistence, and a willingness to learn, you can overcome any obstacle.
3. Seek Support and Guidance: Reach out to supportive individuals who can offer guidance, encouragement, and a fresh perspective. Surround yourself with a network of like-minded individuals who share your vision and can provide support during challenging times.

C. Practicing Self-Care and Nurturing Motivation Throughout the Journey

Maintaining motivation is crucial for sustaining momentum on your manifestation journey. Practicing self-care helps nurture your motivation and overall well-being:

1. Self-Care Rituals: Engage in activities that rejuvenate and uplift you. This can include meditation, exercise, spending time in nature, engaging in creative pursuits, or practicing gratitude. Taking care of your physical, emotional, and mental well-being allows you to stay motivated and focused.
2. Celebrate Small Wins: Acknowledge and celebrate your progress, no matter how small. Recognize and appreciate the steps you've taken towards your intentions. Celebrating small wins fuels your motivation and reinforces your belief in the manifestation process.
3. Regularly Revisit Your Intentions: Stay connected to your intentions by regularly revisiting them. Remind yourself of the reasons why you set those intentions and the vision you have for your life. Visualize the realization of your desires and reinforce your belief in their manifestation.

Summary
Maintaining focus and resilience are essential elements in the manifestation journey. By implementing strategies to stay focused amidst distractions and challenges, building resilience in the face of setbacks, and practicing self-care to nurture motivation, you strengthen your ability to manifest your intentions. Remember that setbacks are temporary, and with persistence and self-care, you can overcome them. In the next section, we will explore the role of gratitude and its impact on the manifestation process in *Setting Clear Intentions*.

Part 7: Reviewing and Revising Your Intentions

Setting Clear Intentions is a powerful step towards manifesting your desires. However, as you progress on your journey, it's important to regularly review and revise your intentions to ensure they align with your evolving aspirations. In this section, we will explore the significance of regularly assessing your progress, reflecting on lessons learned, celebrating achievements, and continuously aligning your intentions with your ever-changing aspirations.

A. Regularly Assessing Progress and Adjusting Intentions if Needed

Regularly assessing your progress is essential to ensure that your intentions are still aligned with your desired outcomes. Life is dynamic, and as you grow and evolve, your aspirations may change. Here's how you can assess your progress and make necessary adjustments:

1. Self-Reflection: Take time to reflect on your journey so far. Evaluate your achievements, challenges, and the alignment between your current reality and your intentions. Ask yourself if your intentions still resonate with your deepest desires and if any adjustments are necessary.

2. Check-in with Your Inner Guidance: Tune into your intuition and listen to your inner voice. It can provide valuable insights and guidance regarding the alignment of your intentions. Trust your intuition and be open to adjusting your intentions based on its wisdom.

3. Recognize Opportunities for Growth: Identify areas where you can enhance your intentions or set new ones that align with your personal growth and aspirations. Assess whether your intentions are still challenging enough to inspire growth while remaining realistic and attainable.

B. Reflecting on Lessons Learned and Celebrating Achievements

Reflection is a powerful tool for personal growth and manifestation. Take time to reflect on the lessons learned along your journey and celebrate your achievements, no matter how small. Here's how you can incorporate reflection and celebration into your practice:

1. Journaling: Maintain a journal dedicated to your manifestation journey. Regularly write about your experiences, insights, and lessons learned. Capture moments of gratitude for the progress you have made and celebrate your achievements.

2. Gratitude Practice: Cultivate a gratitude practice to acknowledge and appreciate the manifestations and progress you have experienced. Expressing gratitude

for what you have already attracted into your life amplifies positive energy and reinforces your belief in the manifestation process.

3. Milestone Celebrations: Set milestones along your journey and celebrate each one as you reach them. This can be as simple as treating yourself to something special, sharing your achievements with loved ones, or engaging in a meaningful self-care activity.

C. Continuously Aligning Intentions with Evolving Aspirations

As you grow and your aspirations evolve, it's important to align your intentions with your new vision. This ongoing alignment ensures that your intentions remain in harmony with your deepest desires. Here's how you can continuously align your intentions:

1. Vision Board Updates: If you have a vision board or visual representation of your goals, regularly update it to reflect your evolving aspirations. Add new images, words, or symbols that represent your expanded vision and desires.

2. Affirmation Refinement: Review and revise your affirmations to ensure they reflect your current aspirations and mindset. Refine your affirmations to align with your evolving beliefs and goals.

3. Stay Open to Inspiration: Remain open to new insights and inspiration that may guide you towards refining or expanding your intentions. Be receptive to opportunities and synchronicities that present themselves along your journey, as they may provide valuable clues for realignment.

Summary

Regularly reviewing and revising your intentions is an important aspect of the manifestation process. By assessing your progress, reflecting on lessons learned, celebrating achievements, and aligning your intentions with your evolving aspirations, you ensure that your manifestation practice remains in harmony with your deepest desires. In the next section, we will explore the role of gratitude and its impact on *Setting Clear Intentions*.

Conclusion: Setting Clear Intentions

Setting Clear Intentions is a transformative practice that empowers you to navigate your path to success. By understanding the power of intentions, clarifying your desires and goals, writing, and affirming your intentions, strengthening your belief and alignment, taking inspired action, maintaining focus and resilience, and reviewing and revising your intentions, you harness the energy of manifestation and create a powerful momentum towards achieving your dreams.

Throughout this chapter, we have explored the significance of aligning your thoughts and emotions in manifestation and the role that intentions play in shaping your thoughts, actions, and ultimately, your reality. We have delved into the process of clarifying your desires, setting specific goals, and creating visual representations to anchor your intentions firmly in your consciousness.

Writing and affirming your intentions using clear and positive language, while staying present and focused, further enhances the power of your intentions. By regularly revisiting and reinforcing your intentions, you maintain a strong belief in their realization and overcome doubts and limiting beliefs that may arise.

Taking inspired action is a vital step in turning your intentions into tangible results. By identifying actionable tasks and milestones, as well as embracing opportunities and acting on your intuition, you propel yourself forward on your path to success.

To sustain your journey, it is crucial to maintain focus amidst distractions, cultivate resilience in the face of setbacks, and prioritize self-care to nurture your motivation. By practicing mindfulness and incorporating self-reflection, gratitude, and celebration into your routine, you stay connected to your intentions and maintain the alignment necessary for manifestation.

Finally, regularly reviewing and revising your intentions ensures that they remain in alignment with your evolving aspirations. By assessing your progress, reflecting on lessons learned, and realigning your intentions with your current vision, you stay attuned to the changes within yourself and adapt your manifestation practice accordingly.

As you continue your path to success, remember that *Setting Clear Intentions* is a dynamic and ongoing process. It requires dedication, self-awareness, and a willingness to adapt. By harnessing the energy of manifestation through intentional thoughts, aligned emotions, and inspired action, you have the power to create the life you desire.

So, take the knowledge and insights gained from this chapter and embark on your journey with confidence. Trust in the process, believe in your abilities, and stay committed to *Setting Clear Intentions* that align with your deepest desires. Embrace the transformative power of manifestation and watch as your dreams manifest into reality.

The journey continues, and the next chapter awaits your exploration. Get ready to dive into the realm of gratitude and its profound impact on aligning your thoughts and emotions for manifestation.

Chapter 6: Overcoming Limiting Beliefs: Rewriting Your Subconscious Mind

Welcome to the chapter on "Overcoming Limiting Beliefs: Rewriting Your Subconscious Mind." In our journey towards personal growth and success, there is a powerful force that often holds us back—the influence of our limiting beliefs. These beliefs, deeply embedded in our subconscious mind, can shape our thoughts, emotions, and actions, and ultimately determine the outcomes we experience in life.

Addressing and *Overcoming Limiting Beliefs* is of paramount importance for our personal growth and success. These beliefs act as invisible barriers that hinder our progress, preventing us from reaching our true potential. They are the product of past experiences, conditioning, and societal influences, often leading us to doubt our abilities, undermine our worth, and limit our aspirations.

By actively identifying and challenging these limiting beliefs, we can unlock new possibilities, expand our horizons, and create a foundation for personal growth and success. It is through this process of rewriting our subconscious mind that we can break free from the shackles of self-imposed limitations and pave the way for a more fulfilling and empowered life.

Throughout this chapter, we will explore various aspects of *Overcoming Limiting Beliefs* and rewiring our subconscious mind. We will delve into the origins and impact of limiting beliefs, understand how they shape our perception of ourselves and the world, and learn effective strategies to challenge and reframe these beliefs.

Our journey will involve self-reflection, questioning the validity of our beliefs, and adopting empowering perspectives. We will explore techniques for healing and releasing emotional attachments to limiting beliefs, as well as practical approaches to reprogram the subconscious mind with empowering thoughts and beliefs.

Additionally, we will discuss the importance of maintaining a positive mindset, building resilience, and continuously evolving in the face of challenges. By the end of this chapter, you will have a comprehensive toolkit to overcome limiting beliefs, rewrite your subconscious mind, and embark on a transformative journey towards personal growth and success.

So, let us begin this empowering exploration of *Overcoming Limiting Beliefs* and rewiring your subconscious mind. Get ready to unlock your true potential and create a life that aligns with your deepest aspirations and dreams.

Part 1: Understanding Limiting Beliefs

In our journey to overcome limiting beliefs and unlock our full potential, it is crucial to first understand the nature and impact of these beliefs. Limiting beliefs are deeply ingrained thoughts and perceptions that hold us back from realizing our true capabilities and achieving our goals. They shape our thoughts, influence our emotions, and dictate our actions, often leading us to settle for less than we deserve. In this section, we will explore the definition of limiting beliefs and how they are formed, shedding light on their profound influence on our subconscious mind.

A. Definition of Limiting Beliefs and Their Impact on Thoughts, Emotions, and Actions

Limiting beliefs can be defined as deeply held convictions or assumptions that constrain our thinking and limit our potential. They are negative or self-defeating beliefs that create barriers in various aspects of our lives, such as relationships, career, health, and personal growth. These beliefs stem from past experiences, conditioning, and societal influences, shaping our perception of ourselves and the world around us.

The impact of limiting beliefs is far-reaching. They infiltrate our thoughts, often manifesting as self-doubt, self-criticism, and a fear of failure. They generate negative emotions such as anxiety, insecurity, and frustration, hindering our confidence and motivation. Moreover, limiting beliefs influence our actions by causing us to play it safe, avoid risks, and stay within our comfort zones, preventing us from seizing opportunities and reaching our true potential.

To overcome limiting beliefs, it is essential to recognize their pervasive influence and the ways in which they shape our thoughts, emotions, and actions. By gaining awareness of these beliefs and their impact, we can begin the transformative journey towards rewriting our subconscious mind.

B. How Limiting Beliefs Are Formed and Their Role in Shaping the Subconscious Mind

Limiting beliefs are often formed through a combination of experiences, observations, and internalization of external influences. During our upbringing and interactions with others, we absorb beliefs and messages that shape our perception of ourselves and the world. These can include societal norms, cultural expectations, parental guidance, and past failures or rejections.

Once these beliefs are internalized, they become deeply embedded in our subconscious mind. The subconscious mind acts as a reservoir of thoughts, memories, and beliefs that influence our daily thoughts, emotions, and actions. It operates beneath our conscious awareness, yet it exerts a powerful influence on our behaviors and choices.

Limiting beliefs, residing within the subconscious mind, become automatic thought patterns that dictate our perception of what is possible for us. They create a filter through which we interpret the world, reinforcing a negative self-image and inhibiting our growth and success. However, by understanding the role of limiting beliefs in shaping the subconscious mind, we gain the power to challenge and rewrite these beliefs, paving the way for personal transformation and liberation.

Summary
Understanding limiting beliefs is the first step in the journey of overcoming them. We have explored the definition and impact of these beliefs on our thoughts, emotions, and actions. Additionally, we have recognized how limiting beliefs are formed and their significant role in shaping our subconscious mind. Armed with this knowledge, we can embark on the path of self-discovery and empowerment, ready to challenge and overcome the limitations that have held us back. In the following sections, we will delve deeper into strategies and techniques to effectively overcome limiting beliefs and rewrite our subconscious mind for a more fulfilling and successful life.

Part 2: Identifying Your Limiting Beliefs

In our quest to overcome limiting beliefs, it is essential to first identify and understand the specific beliefs that hold us back. This process of self-reflection and introspection allows us to uncover hidden beliefs, recognize common themes and patterns, and gain awareness of their impact on various aspects of our lives. In this section, we will explore strategies to identify and shed light on our limiting beliefs, paving the way for their transformation and eventual overcoming.

A. Self-Reflection and Introspection to Uncover Hidden Beliefs

Self-reflection and introspection serve as valuable tools for uncovering the deep-seated beliefs that reside within us. Taking time for self-examination allows us to delve into our thoughts, emotions, and experiences, unveiling the beliefs that shape our perception of ourselves and the world. It involves asking ourselves probing questions and being open to honest self-assessment.

During this process, it is important to pay attention to recurring thoughts, self-critical narratives, and emotional triggers. By observing our inner dialogue and reflecting on our reactions to certain situations, we can gain insight into the underlying beliefs that drive our behaviors and choices.

B. Common Themes and Patterns in Limiting Beliefs

While each person's limiting beliefs are unique, there are often common themes and patterns that arise. These themes may revolve around worthiness, success, relationships, abundance, or personal abilities. For example, some common limiting beliefs include "I am not good enough," "I don't deserve happiness," or "I will never succeed."

By exploring these common themes, we can identify shared beliefs that may be holding us back collectively. Recognizing that we are not alone in grappling with these limiting beliefs can be reassuring and provide a sense of unity and support in our journey of overcoming them.

C. Recognizing the Impact of Limiting Beliefs on Various Areas of Life

Limiting beliefs have a pervasive impact on different areas of our lives. They affect our relationships, career choices, financial decisions, health behaviors, and personal growth. By recognizing the influence of these beliefs, we can gain a clearer understanding of how they create barriers and hinder our progress.

In relationships, for instance, limiting beliefs can lead to self-sabotage, fear of vulnerability, or an inability to trust others fully. In our careers, they may manifest as imposter syndrome, a fear of taking risks, or a reluctance to pursue new opportunities. By examining the impact of limiting beliefs across various domains, we can comprehensively address their influence and work towards their transformation.

Summary

Identifying our limiting beliefs is a crucial step on the path to overcoming them. Through self-reflection and introspection, we can uncover the hidden beliefs that hold us back. By recognizing common themes and patterns, we gain a broader understanding of the shared struggles we may face. Additionally, by acknowledging the impact of these beliefs on different areas of our lives, we develop a comprehensive perspective on the changes needed for personal growth.

In the following sections, we will explore practical strategies and techniques to effectively overcome limiting beliefs and rewrite our subconscious mind. By shining a light on our limiting beliefs and understanding their influence, we pave the way for transformation, self-empowerment, and a renewed sense of possibility.

Part 3: Challenging and Reframing Limiting Beliefs

Once we have identified our limiting beliefs, the next step is to challenge and reframe them. This process involves questioning the validity and evidence of these beliefs, replacing negative self-talk with empowering affirmations, and utilizing cognitive restructuring techniques. By actively engaging in this transformative work, we can gradually shift our mindset and free ourselves from the constraints of limiting beliefs. In this section, we will explore practical strategies to challenge and reframe these beliefs, empowering ourselves to overcome them and embrace a more positive and empowering perspective.

A. Questioning the Validity and Evidence of Limiting Beliefs

To overcome limiting beliefs, it is essential to question their validity and the evidence supporting them. Often, these beliefs are based on past experiences, self-perceptions, or societal conditioning. However, they may not necessarily reflect the truth or be grounded in objective reality.

By examining the basis of our limiting beliefs, we can challenge their accuracy and challenge the assumptions underlying them. We can ask ourselves critical questions such as, "What evidence do I have to support this belief?" or "Is there an alternative perspective or counterexample that challenges this belief?" Through this process of inquiry, we begin to dismantle the foundation of our limiting beliefs and open ourselves up to new possibilities.

B. Replacing Negative Self-Talk with Empowering Affirmations

Negative self-talk reinforces our limiting beliefs and keeps us trapped in a cycle of self-doubt and negativity. To counteract this, it is important to replace negative self-talk with empowering affirmations. Affirmations are positive statements that help us reprogram our subconscious mind and reinforce new, empowering beliefs.

By consciously choosing affirmations that counter our limiting beliefs and repeating them regularly, we can gradually shift our internal dialogue and strengthen more positive and empowering thought patterns. For example, if our limiting belief is "I am not capable of success," we can replace it with affirmations such as "I am capable of achieving my goals" or "I have the skills and determination to succeed." These affirmations serve as powerful reminders of our inherent abilities and potential.

C. Cognitive Restructuring Techniques to Reframe Limiting Beliefs

Cognitive restructuring techniques help us reframe our limiting beliefs by challenging and replacing them with more empowering thoughts. These techniques involve identifying cognitive distortions, reframing negative thoughts, and adopting alternative perspectives.

One effective cognitive restructuring technique is reframing. It involves consciously shifting our perspective to view a situation or belief in a more positive or realistic light. For example, if our limiting belief is "I always fail at new challenges," we can reframe it by acknowledging past successes and focusing on the lessons learned from perceived failures.

Another technique is evidence gathering, where we actively seek evidence that contradicts our limiting beliefs. By consciously seeking counterexamples, we challenge the validity of our beliefs and open ourselves up to alternative possibilities.

Summary
Challenging and reframing our limiting beliefs is a powerful
process that enables us to break free from their constraints
and embrace a more empowering mindset. By questioning the
validity and evidence of our limiting beliefs, replacing
negative self-talk with affirmations, and utilizing cognitive
restructuring techniques, we actively work towards
transforming our subconscious mind.

Through these practices, we can gradually release the grip of
limiting beliefs and open ourselves up to new opportunities
and possibilities. *Overcoming Limiting Beliefs* is an ongoing
journey, but by engaging in these transformative strategies,
we empower ourselves to rewrite our subconscious mind and
create a more positive and fulfilling life.

Part 4: Healing and Releasing Limiting Beliefs

Healing and releasing limiting beliefs is a crucial step in the
journey of overcoming them. These beliefs often carry an
emotional charge that keeps us stuck in patterns of self-doubt
and fear. To truly liberate ourselves from their grip, we must
engage in emotional healing and processing, practice
forgiveness and letting go, and seek support from trusted
resources. In this section, we will explore strategies for
healing and releasing limiting beliefs, empowering ourselves
to create positive change and embrace our true potential.

A. Emotional Healing and Processing to Release the Emotional Charge

Limiting beliefs are not just intellectual constructs; they are
intertwined with our emotions. The emotional charge
associated with these beliefs can be significant and impact our
self-esteem, confidence, and overall well-being. To overcome
limiting beliefs, it is essential to engage in emotional healing
and processing.

This process involves acknowledging and exploring the
emotions tied to our limiting beliefs. By allowing ourselves to
feel and express these emotions, we create space for healing
and release. Techniques such as journaling, meditation, or
talking to a trusted friend or therapist can support us in this
journey. Through emotional healing and processing, we can

gradually reduce the emotional intensity associated with our limiting beliefs and pave the way for positive transformation.

B. Forgiveness and Letting Go of Past Experiences
Limiting beliefs often stem from past experiences that have reinforced negative narratives about ourselves. To release these beliefs, it is crucial to practice forgiveness and let go of the pain and resentment associated with those experiences.

Forgiveness does not mean condoning or forgetting the past; rather, it is a conscious choice to release ourselves from the burden of carrying resentments and grudges. By forgiving ourselves and others, we free up energy and create space for new beliefs and possibilities. Letting go involves releasing the grip of the past and embracing the present moment with openness and acceptance.

C. Seeking Support Through Therapy, Coaching, or Personal Development Resources
Overcoming Limiting Beliefs can be a challenging journey, and seeking support can provide invaluable guidance and encouragement. Therapists, coaches, or personal development resources can offer insights, tools, and techniques tailored to our specific needs.

Therapy can help us explore the roots of our limiting beliefs, process past traumas, and develop coping strategies. Coaches can provide accountability, guidance, and empower us to challenge and overcome our limitations. Personal development resources, such as books, workshops, or online courses, can also provide valuable insights and practical exercises to support our growth.

Summary
Healing and releasing limiting beliefs is a transformative process that requires emotional healing, forgiveness, and seeking support. By engaging in emotional healing and processing, we can release the emotional charge associated with our limiting beliefs. Practicing forgiveness and letting go allows us to free ourselves from the weight of the past and create space for new beliefs. Seeking support through

therapy, coaching, or personal development resources provides valuable guidance and tools to navigate this journey.

By actively participating in these healing and releasing practices, we empower ourselves to let go of the limitations that hold us back and embrace a new narrative of possibility and growth. *Overcoming Limiting Beliefs* requires dedication and self-compassion, but the rewards are immense. As we heal and release our limiting beliefs, we step into our true potential and open ourselves up to a life filled with confidence, fulfillment, and purpose.

Part 5: Reprogramming the Subconscious Mind

Reprogramming the subconscious mind is a powerful tool in *Overcoming Limiting Beliefs*. Our subconscious mind plays a significant role in shaping our thoughts, emotions, and actions, and by harnessing its potential, we can create positive shifts in our beliefs and behaviors. In this section, we will explore techniques for reprogramming the subconscious mind, including visualization, hypnosis, consistent practice, repetition, and the power of affirmations. By actively engaging in these practices, we can overwrite limiting beliefs and foster a mindset of empowerment and possibility.

A. Techniques for Reprogramming the Subconscious Mind

- Visualization: Visualization is a technique that involves creating vivid mental images of desired outcomes and experiences. By consistently visualizing ourselves as confident, capable, and successful, we send powerful messages to our subconscious mind. This practice helps to align our beliefs and actions with our desired reality, gradually replacing limiting beliefs with empowering ones.
- Hypnosis: Hypnosis is a state of focused attention and heightened suggestibility. Through guided hypnosis sessions or self-hypnosis techniques, we can access the subconscious mind and introduce positive suggestions and affirmations. This process allows us to bypass the critical conscious mind and directly influence our subconscious beliefs, facilitating profound shifts in our thinking and behavior.

B. Consistent Practice and Repetition

Reprogramming the subconscious mind requires consistent practice and repetition. Our beliefs are deeply ingrained, and it takes time and dedication to overwrite limiting patterns. By consistently engaging in the techniques mentioned above, we reinforce new positive beliefs and weaken the influence of limiting ones.

Regular practice helps to create new neural pathways in the brain, strengthening the connection between empowering thoughts and desired outcomes. Repetition is key to reprogramming the subconscious mind, as it allows the new beliefs to become deeply rooted and automatic. By persistently and consistently working with these techniques, we gradually reshape our subconscious programming and open ourselves up to new possibilities.

C. Harnessing the Power of Affirmations and Self-Affirming Statements

Affirmations are positive statements that help to reframe our beliefs and reinforce new, empowering narratives. By consciously choosing affirmations that counteract our limiting beliefs, we can gradually shift our subconscious programming. Affirmations should be stated in the present tense, using positive language and personal pronouns, and should evoke a sense of emotion and belief.

Repeating affirmations daily, whether silently or aloud, helps to embed them into our subconscious mind. Alongside affirmations, self-affirming statements can be used to challenge and replace negative self-talk. By consistently affirming our worth, capabilities, and potential, we gradually build a strong foundation of self-belief and resilience.

Summary

Reprogramming the subconscious mind is a powerful process in *Overcoming Limiting Beliefs*. By utilizing techniques such as visualization and hypnosis, engaging in consistent practice and repetition, and harnessing the power of affirmations and self-affirming statements, we can actively reshape our subconscious programming. Over time, these practices help to overwrite limiting beliefs and cultivate a mindset of empowerment and possibility.

As we commit to reprogramming our subconscious mind, it is important to approach these practices with patience, consistency, and self-compassion. Each small step we take in the direction of reprogramming our subconscious contributes to our personal growth and transformation. By persistently working with these techniques, we pave the way for new beliefs, expanded possibilities, and a life lived beyond the limitations of our old subconscious programming.

Part 6: Cultivating Empowering Beliefs

Cultivating empowering beliefs is a crucial step in *Overcoming Limiting Beliefs* and creating a mindset of possibility and growth. Our beliefs shape our perception of ourselves, others, and the world around us. By consciously cultivating empowering beliefs, we open ourselves up to new opportunities, embrace personal development, and create a positive foundation for achieving our goals. In this section, we will explore strategies for cultivating empowering beliefs, including embracing a growth mindset, adopting empowering beliefs aligned with our aspirations, and surrounding ourselves with positive influences and supportive environments.

A. Embracing a Growth Mindset

A growth mindset is the belief that our abilities and intelligence can be developed through dedication, effort, and learning. By embracing a growth mindset, we recognize that our potential is not fixed and that we have the power to improve and evolve over time. This mindset shift allows us to view challenges as opportunities for growth, setbacks as learning experiences, and failures as stepping stones to success. By cultivating a growth mindset, we challenge the limitations imposed by our limiting beliefs and open ourselves up to the possibility of continuous improvement and personal development.

B. Adopting Empowering Beliefs

Adopting empowering beliefs involves consciously choosing beliefs that support our goals, aspirations, and values. Instead of allowing limiting beliefs to hold us back, we actively replace them with empowering narratives. For example, if we hold a belief that we are not capable of success, we can reframe it as "I am capable of achieving my goals with persistence and effort." By adopting empowering beliefs, we align our thoughts, emotions, and actions with our desired outcomes, creating a positive mindset that propels us forward.

C. Surrounding Yourself with Positive Influences and Supportive Environments

The people we surround ourselves with and the environments we immerse ourselves in have a profound impact on our beliefs and mindset. To cultivate empowering beliefs, it is essential to surround ourselves with positive influences and supportive environments. Seek out individuals who uplift and inspire you, who believe in your potential, and who embody the qualities and values you aspire to. Additionally, create an environment that nurtures your growth and supports your journey. This may involve surrounding yourself with positive affirmations, engaging in personal development activities, or seeking out communities and resources that align with your aspirations.

Summary

Cultivating empowering beliefs is a transformative process in *Overcoming Limiting Beliefs* and embracing personal growth. By embracing a growth mindset, adopting empowering beliefs, and surrounding ourselves with positive influences and supportive environments, we create a fertile ground for personal development and achievement. It is through conscious choice and consistent practice that we reshape our beliefs and nurture a mindset of possibility and empowerment. As we continue our journey of *Overcoming Limiting Beliefs*, let us remember the power of cultivating empowering beliefs and the tremendous impact they can have on our lives.

Part 7: Maintaining a Positive Mindset

Maintaining a positive mindset is essential in the journey of *Overcoming Limiting Beliefs*. While we work on reframing our beliefs and cultivating empowering thoughts, it is natural to face self-doubt and encounter setbacks along the way.

However, by employing effective strategies for managing self-doubt, building resilience, and embracing continuous growth, we can maintain a positive mindset that propels us forward. In this section, we will explore strategies to maintain a positive mindset throughout the process of *Overcoming Limiting Beliefs*.

A. Strategies for Managing Self-Doubt and Setbacks
Self-doubt often creeps in when we are challenging and transforming our limiting beliefs. To manage self-doubt, it is important to practice self-awareness and recognize when negative self-talk arises. When self-doubt surfaces, remind yourself of the progress you have made so far in *Overcoming Limiting Beliefs* and the empowering beliefs you have adopted. Reframe self-doubt as an opportunity for growth and view it as a natural part of the process. Additionally, seek support from trusted individuals who can provide encouragement and perspective, and remember to celebrate even the smallest victories along the way.

Setbacks are also common on the path of *Overcoming Limiting Beliefs*. Instead of viewing setbacks as failures or reasons to give up, see them as valuable learning experiences. Embrace setbacks as opportunities to refine your approach, learn new strategies, and grow stronger. Maintain a growth mindset and remind yourself that setbacks are temporary and part of the journey toward personal growth and transformation. Learn from setbacks, adjust your course if necessary, and keep moving forward with determination.

B. Building Resilience and Practicing Self-Compassion
Building resilience is crucial when facing challenges in the process of *Overcoming Limiting Beliefs*. Resilience allows us to bounce back from setbacks, maintain our motivation, and stay focused on our goals. Cultivate resilience by cultivating a positive support system, practicing self-care, and engaging in activities that recharge and rejuvenate you. Take time to rest and recharge, engage in activities that bring you joy and fulfillment, and prioritize self-care practices that nurture your overall well-being.

In addition to building resilience, practicing self-compassion is vital. Acknowledge that challenging and transforming limiting beliefs is a courageous and challenging journey. Treat yourself with kindness and understanding. Embrace the imperfections and setbacks as opportunities for growth rather than reasons for self-criticism. Be patient with yourself and recognize that it takes time and effort to rewire deeply ingrained beliefs. Practice self-compassion by offering yourself words of encouragement and embracing self-love throughout the process.

C. Continuous Growth and Evolution

Overcoming Limiting Beliefs is not a one-time event but a continuous process of growth and evolution. As you challenge and transform your limiting beliefs, embrace the idea that personal growth is an ongoing journey. Remain open to new insights, experiences, and perspectives that can further expand your understanding and help you transcend limitations. Continuously seek opportunities for growth, whether it's through further education, seeking out mentors or coaches, or exploring personal development resources. Embrace the mindset of continuous learning and evolution, knowing that as you overcome limiting beliefs, you create space for new beliefs and possibilities to emerge.

Summary

Maintaining a positive mindset is a vital aspect of *Overcoming Limiting Beliefs*. By employing strategies to manage self-doubt and setbacks, building resilience, and embracing continuous growth, we nurture a positive mindset that supports our journey of transformation. Remember that setbacks and self-doubt are part of the process and can serve as catalysts for growth. With self-compassion and a growth-oriented mindset, we can maintain a positive outlook, stay motivated, and continue the journey of *Overcoming Limiting Beliefs* with determination and resilience.

Conclusion: Overcoming Limiting Beliefs

Overcoming Limiting Beliefs and rewriting your subconscious mind is a powerful journey of self-discovery and personal transformation. Throughout this chapter, we have explored the significance of addressing limiting beliefs, identifying, and challenging them, healing and releasing their emotional charge, reprogramming the subconscious mind, cultivating empowering beliefs, and maintaining a positive mindset.

Limiting beliefs have a profound impact on our thoughts, emotions, and actions, often holding us back from reaching our full potential. By understanding the nature of these beliefs and their origins, we can begin the process of liberation and self-growth. Through self-reflection and introspection, we uncover hidden beliefs and recognize their influence on various areas of our lives.

Challenging and reframing limiting beliefs involves questioning their validity and replacing negative self-talk with empowering affirmations. By consciously restructuring our thoughts and adopting new perspectives, we create fertile ground for positive change. Healing and releasing limiting beliefs requires emotional processing, forgiveness, and seeking support when needed. By acknowledging and letting go of past experiences that reinforce these beliefs, we create space for healing and personal growth.

Reprogramming the subconscious mind is a crucial step in *Overcoming Limiting Beliefs*. Techniques such as visualization, hypnosis, and consistent practice help to reinforce positive beliefs and overwrite the limiting ones. Affirmations, self-affirming statements, and surrounding ourselves with positive influences contribute to the rewiring process, supporting our journey towards transformation.

Cultivating empowering beliefs is essential for long-term change. By adopting a growth mindset, embracing change, and surrounding ourselves with positive influences, we create an environment that nurtures our aspirations and supports our goals.

Maintaining a positive mindset throughout the process is vital. Strategies such as managing self-doubt, building resilience, practicing self-compassion, and embracing continuous growth help us stay focused, motivated, and resilient in the face of challenges.

In the pursuit of rewriting our subconscious mind, we embark on a continuous journey of growth and evolution. By regularly reviewing and revisiting our beliefs, assessing our progress, and adjusting our intentions, we align ourselves with our evolving aspirations and create a solid foundation for personal success.

Remember, the journey of *Overcoming Limiting Beliefs* is not without its obstacles, but with determination, self-compassion, and a belief in your own potential, you can rewrite your subconscious mind and create a life aligned with your true desires. Embrace the power within you, trust in the process, and know that by rewriting your subconscious mind, you open the doors to endless possibilities and a life filled with fulfillment and joy.

Discover the transformative journey of *Overcoming Limiting Beliefs* and rewiring your subconscious mind to unlock your full potential and create a life of empowerment and fulfillment.

Chapter 7: Cultivating Gratitude and Abundance: Opening the Floodgates of Manifestation

Welcome to the chapter on "Cultivating Gratitude and Abundance: Opening the Floodgates of Manifestation." In this chapter, we will explore the profound impact that gratitude and abundance can have on our ability to manifest our desires and create a life of fulfillment and joy.

Gratitude and abundance are not just fleeting emotions or distant concepts; they are powerful forces that can shape our reality. When we cultivate a mindset of gratitude, we open ourselves up to receiving more of what we appreciate and value in our lives. It is a way of acknowledging and celebrating the abundance that already exists within and around us.

Manifestation is the process of bringing our desires into reality, and gratitude serves as a catalyst for this process. By recognizing and expressing gratitude for what we already have, we shift our focus from scarcity to abundance. This shift in perspective allows us to tap into the limitless possibilities and opportunities that surround us.

Throughout this chapter, we will delve into various aspects of cultivating gratitude and abundance in our lives. We will explore practical techniques and strategies that can help us develop gratitude practice and embrace an abundant mindset. By doing so, we can open the floodgates of manifestation and create the life we truly desire.

First, we will examine the concept of gratitude in detail, understanding its definition and the profound impact it can have on our mindset and overall well-being. We will explore how gratitude acts as a powerful magnet for attracting abundance into our lives.

Next, we will dive into practical ways to practice gratitude. From daily rituals and gratitude journaling to finding gratitude in challenging situations, we will uncover actionable steps that can help us infuse gratitude into every aspect of our lives.

We will then shift our focus to embracing abundance. We will explore the shift from a scarcity mindset to an abundance mindset and discover how to recognize and appreciate the abundance that already exists in our lives. Through affirmations, visualizations, and intentional practices, we can amplify our sense of abundance and attract more of it into our reality.

Furthermore, we will explore the relationship between gratitude, abundance, and our connections with others. We will learn how to nurture gratitude in relationships and express abundance through acts of kindness, fostering a positive and supportive environment for manifestation.

As we progress, we will delve into the manifestation process itself. We will discuss how to set intentions with a grateful and abundant mindset, align our thoughts, emotions, and actions with gratitude and abundance, and surrender to the flow of manifestation with trust and gratitude.

Challenges are a natural part of life, and we will address how to overcome them while maintaining a grateful and abundant perspective. Building resilience and a positive mindset will be key in navigating obstacles and staying aligned with gratitude and abundance.

Finally, we will explore how to cultivate a gratitude and abundance lifestyle that extends beyond mere practices. We will discuss integrating gratitude and abundance into our daily lives, creating a supportive environment, and sustaining a consistent practice to manifest our desires in the long run.

Get ready to embark on a transformative journey of cultivating gratitude and abundance and witness the floodgates of manifestation opening before you. Through the power of gratitude and an abundance mindset, you have the potential to create a life filled with joy, fulfillment, and endless possibilities. Let's dive in!

Part 1: Understanding Gratitude

Before we can fully cultivate gratitude and abundance in our lives, it is essential to understand the true meaning and significance of gratitude. In this section, we will explore what gratitude is, how it impacts our mindset and well-being, and its role in manifesting abundance.

A. Definition and Significance of Gratitude

Gratitude is a deep sense of appreciation and thankfulness for the blessings, experiences, and people in our lives. It goes beyond a simple "thank you" and involves recognizing and acknowledging the goodness that exists within and around us. Gratitude allows us to shift our focus from what is lacking to what is present, nurturing a positive perspective and a sense of contentment.

The significance of gratitude lies in its transformative power. When we embrace gratitude, we become aware of the abundance that already exists in our lives, no matter how small or seemingly insignificant. It is through gratitude that we can find joy, peace, and fulfillment in the present moment, rather than constantly chasing future desires.

B. How Gratitude Affects Our Mindset and Well-Being

Gratitude has a profound impact on our mindset and overall well-being. When we cultivate a practice of gratitude, our mindset shifts from one of scarcity to one of abundance. Instead of focusing on what we lack or what is going wrong, gratitude directs our attention towards what we have and what is going well.

This shift in mindset brings about a multitude of benefits. Gratitude enhances our sense of happiness and satisfaction, as it allows us to appreciate the positive aspects of our lives. It also improves our mental and emotional well-being by reducing stress, anxiety, and negative thinking. Practicing gratitude regularly can even strengthen our relationships, as we become more attuned to the kindness and support we receive from others.

C. The Role of Gratitude in Manifesting Abundance

Gratitude plays a vital role in the manifestation of abundance. When we approach life with a grateful heart, we open ourselves up to receiving more blessings and opportunities. Gratitude serves as a powerful magnet, attracting more of what we appreciate and value into our lives.

By expressing gratitude for what we already have, we create a positive energy that aligns us with the frequency of abundance. This alignment allows us to tap into the limitless possibilities and opportunities that exist in the universe. When we cultivate gratitude and truly believe in the abundance available to us, we create a fertile ground for manifesting our desires.

In essence, gratitude and abundance go hand in hand. The more we practice gratitude, the more abundance we attract. And the more abundance we experience, the more reasons we find to be grateful. It is a beautiful cycle that perpetuates positivity, fulfillment, and the manifestation of our deepest desires.

Summary

Understanding gratitude is the first step in cultivating a life filled with gratitude and abundance. By recognizing the definition and significance of gratitude, acknowledging its impact on our mindset and well-being, and understanding its role in manifesting abundance, we lay a strong foundation for the transformative power of gratitude to unfold in our lives. In the next sections, we will explore practical techniques and strategies to cultivate gratitude and embrace abundance, enabling us to open the floodgates of manifestation and create a life of joy, fulfillment, and endless possibilities.

Part 2: Practicing Gratitude

Now that we have an understanding of gratitude and its significance in cultivating abundance, let's delve into the practical aspects of practicing gratitude. In this section, we will explore various techniques and exercises to incorporate gratitude into our daily lives, including rituals, journaling, and navigating challenging situations with a grateful mindset.

A. Daily Gratitude Practices and Rituals

Cultivating gratitude begins with making it a part of our daily routine. Engaging in simple gratitude practices and rituals can have a profound impact on our mindset and overall well-being. Start your day by setting the intention to be grateful and make a conscious effort to notice and appreciate the blessings around you. It could be as simple as expressing gratitude for a good night's sleep, a warm cup of coffee, or the beauty of nature outside your window. Throughout the day, pause and take moments to reflect on what you are grateful for, whether it's the support of loved ones, the opportunities you have, or the lessons learned from challenging experiences. By consistently incorporating these practices into your day, you create a habit of gratitude that amplifies the abundance in your life.

B. Gratitude Journaling and Reflection Exercises

Gratitude journaling is a powerful tool to deepen our practice of gratitude. Set aside a few minutes each day to write down the things you are grateful for. This exercise allows you to reflect on the positive aspects of your life and helps you shift your focus from what is lacking to what is present. Write about specific moments, experiences, or even qualities in yourself and others that you appreciate. As you write, let the feelings of gratitude wash over you, immersing yourself in the emotions of appreciation. Additionally, you can engage in reflection exercises, such as reviewing your journal entries at the end of the week or month, to further reinforce your gratitude practice and remind yourself of the abundance that surrounds you.

C. Cultivating Gratitude in Challenging Situations

Practicing gratitude becomes even more essential during challenging times. When faced with adversity, it can be difficult to find reasons to be grateful. However, shifting our perspective and finding gratitude in these situations can provide immense strength and resilience. Look for lessons or silver linings within the challenges you face, recognizing that they contribute to your growth and development. Seek gratitude in the small moments of positivity, the acts of kindness from others, or the strength and courage you discover within yourself. Embracing gratitude during difficult times can help us navigate through them with grace, and ultimately, lead us to a place of greater abundance and growth.

Summary
Practicing gratitude is a transformative journey that opens the floodgates of manifestation and abundance in our lives. By incorporating daily gratitude practices and rituals, engaging in gratitude journaling and reflection exercises, and cultivating gratitude even in challenging situations, we deepen our connection with the abundance that surrounds us. The more we nurture a grateful mindset, the more we attract and manifest the experiences and opportunities aligned with our desires. In the next section, we will explore strategies for cultivating abundance through a shift in mindset and embracing an abundant worldview.

Part 3: Embracing Abundance
In our journey of cultivating gratitude and abundance, it is essential to shift our mindset from scarcity to abundance. Embracing abundance involves recognizing and appreciating the abundance that already exists in our lives, as well as aligning our thoughts, emotions, and beliefs with a mindset of abundance. In this section, we will explore strategies to shift our mindset, appreciate abundance in all areas of life, and harness the power of abundance affirmations and visualizations.

A. Shifting from a Scarcity Mindset to an Abundance Mindset
A scarcity mindset is characterized by a belief in lack and limitation, focusing on what we don't have or what might go wrong. To embrace abundance, we need to shift our perspective and cultivate an abundance mindset. This involves recognizing that there is enough to go around, that

opportunities are abundant, and that we are deserving of abundance. Start by becoming aware of your thoughts and language, replacing scarcity-based thoughts with thoughts of abundance and possibility. Practice gratitude for what you already have and celebrate the successes and abundance in your life. As you consciously choose to see the world through the lens of abundance, you open yourself up to attract more abundance into your life.

B. Recognizing and Appreciating Abundance in All Areas of Life

Abundance extends beyond material wealth and encompasses various aspects of our lives, including relationships, health, personal growth, and experiences. Take time to reflect on the abundance that exists in these areas. Recognize and appreciate the love and support of your relationships, the opportunities for growth and learning, the beauty of nature, and the simple joys that enrich your daily life. By shifting your focus from what is lacking to what is abundant, you create a mindset that magnetizes more abundance in all areas.

C. Abundance Affirmations and Visualizations

Affirmations and visualizations are powerful tools to reinforce the abundance mindset. Affirmations are positive statements that reflect the reality you desire, reinforcing empowering beliefs about abundance and attracting corresponding experiences. Repeat affirmations such as "I am worthy of abundance," "I attract abundance effortlessly," or "I am open to receive unlimited abundance." Visualizations involve creating vivid mental images of the abundant life you desire. Close your eyes and imagine yourself living in a state of abundance, experiencing the joy, fulfillment, and prosperity that comes with it. Engaging your senses in this visualization exercise enhances the impact. By consistently practicing affirmations and visualizations, you reprogram your subconscious mind to align with abundance and attract opportunities that support your desires.

Summary

Embracing abundance is a transformative shift that allows us to experience the fullness and richness of life. By shifting from a scarcity mindset to an abundance mindset, recognizing and appreciating abundance in all areas of life, and utilizing abundance affirmations and visualizations, we align ourselves with the flow of abundance. The combination of gratitude and abundance creates a powerful synergy that propels us towards manifesting our desires and living a life of fulfillment and prosperity. In the next section, we will explore practical steps to take inspired action and manifest abundance in our lives.

Part 4: Gratitude and Abundance in Relationships

Gratitude and abundance have a profound impact on our relationships, creating a positive and nurturing environment that fosters deeper connections with others. When we cultivate gratitude and embrace abundance in our relationships, we open the floodgates for love, kindness, and joy to flow freely. In this section, we will explore how to nurture gratitude in relationships, foster a sense of abundance in our connections with others, and express gratitude and abundance through acts of kindness.

A. Nurturing Gratitude in Relationships

Gratitude is a powerful catalyst for strengthening and nurturing our relationships. It involves acknowledging and appreciating the presence of others in our lives, recognizing the qualities we admire, and expressing heartfelt gratitude for their support, love, and companionship. Take time to reflect on the positive aspects of your relationships and the ways in which others enhance your life. Communicate your gratitude to them through words, gestures, or thoughtful acts of kindness. By nurturing gratitude in our relationships, we create a positive cycle of appreciation and deepened connection.

B. Fostering a Sense of Abundance in Connections with Others

Fostering a sense of abundance in our connections with others involves cultivating an open and generous mindset. Rather than approaching relationships with a scarcity mentality, where we feel the need to compete or hold back, we embrace the abundance of love, support, and opportunities for growth that relationships can offer. Recognize that there is an abundance of meaningful connections available to us and that each relationship has its unique value. Embrace the diversity and richness of relationships, appreciating the different perspectives and experiences they bring. By fostering an abundance mindset, we create an atmosphere of positivity and mutual growth in our connections with others.

C. Expressing Gratitude and Abundance in Acts of Kindness
Acts of kindness are a beautiful way to express gratitude and abundance in our relationships. Small gestures, such as a genuine compliment, a listening ear, or a random act of kindness, can have a profound impact on others. Look for opportunities to show appreciation and support to the people in your life. Engage in acts of kindness without expecting anything in return, simply out of a genuine desire to contribute to their happiness and well-being. By expressing gratitude and abundance through acts of kindness, we create a ripple effect of positivity and love in our relationships.

Summary
Gratitude and abundance are essential ingredients for nurturing and deepening our relationships. By nurturing gratitude, fostering a sense of abundance, and expressing gratitude and abundance through acts of kindness, we create a positive and harmonious environment in our connections with others. As we cultivate gratitude and abundance in our relationships, we not only enhance the quality of our interactions but also attract more meaningful and fulfilling relationships into our lives. In the next section, we will explore how to manifest abundance in our professional endeavors and contribute to the world in a meaningful way.

Part 5: Manifesting with Gratitude and Abundance
Manifesting with gratitude and abundance is about harnessing the power of positive energy to attract and create the life we desire. When we set intentions, align our thoughts, emotions, and actions, and trust in the flow of manifestations, we open ourselves to endless possibilities and opportunities for growth. In this section, we will explore how to manifest with gratitude and abundance by setting intentions, aligning ourselves with positive energy, and embracing the process with trust and gratitude.

A. Setting Intentions with a Grateful and Abundant Mindset
Setting intentions is the first step towards manifesting our desires. When we set intentions with a grateful and abundant mindset, we shift our focus towards what we want to attract into our lives. Begin by cultivating gratitude for what you already have, appreciating the abundance that surrounds you. Then, set clear and specific intentions for what you desire to manifest, whether it's a new opportunity, a fulfilling relationship, or personal growth. By infusing our intentions with gratitude and abundance, we amplify the positive energy and align ourselves with the vibrations of what we want to attract.

B. Aligning Thoughts, Emotions, and Actions with Gratitude and Abundance
Alignment is crucial in the manifestation process. To align our thoughts, emotions, and actions with gratitude and abundance, we must consciously cultivate positive and empowering beliefs. Notice any negative or limiting thoughts that arise and replace them with thoughts of gratitude, abundance, and possibility. Engage in practices such as visualization, affirmations, and gratitude journaling to reinforce positive beliefs and emotions. Additionally, take inspired action towards your desires, making choices that align with your intentions and values. By aligning our thoughts, emotions, and actions with gratitude and abundance, we create a powerful energetic resonance that accelerates the manifestation process.

C. Allowing Manifestations to Flow with Gratitude and Trust
While taking aligned action is essential, it's equally important to cultivate a sense of trust and surrender. Trust that the universe is working in your favor and that your intentions are being manifested in divine timing. Practice gratitude for the manifestations that are already present in your life and trust that more abundance is on its way. Avoid dwelling on doubts, fears, or impatience, as these can block the flow of manifestations. Instead, cultivate a sense of gratitude, openness, and receptivity, allowing manifestations to flow effortlessly into your life. By combining gratitude and trust, you create a receptive space for miracles to unfold.

Summary
Manifesting with gratitude and abundance is a powerful
process that allows us to tap into the unlimited potential of
the universe. By setting intentions with a grateful and
abundant mindset, aligning our thoughts, emotions, and
actions, and embracing the flow of manifestations with
gratitude and trust, we invite the fulfillment of our desires
into our lives. Remember that the journey of manifestation is
not solely about acquiring material possessions but also about
personal growth, joy, and contributing positively to the world.
In the final section, we will explore ways to integrate
gratitude and abundance into our daily lives, creating a
lasting transformation and a foundation for a fulfilling and
abundant future.

Part 6: Overcoming Challenges and Cultivating Resilience

The journey of manifesting with gratitude and abundance is
not without its challenges. Life may present setbacks,
obstacles, and difficulties along the way. However, it is during
these times that our commitment to gratitude and abundance
becomes even more crucial. In this section, we will explore
strategies to overcome challenges and cultivate resilience by
dealing with setbacks, building a positive mindset, and
utilizing gratitude and abundance as guiding forces.

A. Dealing with Setbacks and Maintaining Gratitude

Setbacks are a natural part of life, and it's important to
approach them with resilience and gratitude. When faced
with setbacks, resist the temptation to dwell on negativity or
self-pity. Instead, shift your focus towards gratitude. Reflect
on what you have learned from the experience, find the silver
linings, and appreciate the growth opportunities it presents.
Cultivating gratitude in the face of setbacks allows us to
maintain a positive perspective and opens the door for new
possibilities to emerge.

B. Building Resilience and Positive Mindset in the Face of Obstacles

Obstacles may arise on our path to manifesting with gratitude
and abundance. Building resilience is essential to navigate
these challenges. Begin by developing a positive mindset that

sees obstacles as opportunities for growth and transformation. Embrace a belief that you have the inner strength and capabilities to overcome any challenge that comes your way. Practice self-care, surround yourself with positive influences, and engage in activities that recharge and uplift you. By nurturing resilience and a positive mindset, you empower yourself to overcome obstacles and continue moving forward on your journey.

C. Using Gratitude and Abundance to Navigate Difficulties
During difficult times, gratitude and abundance can serve as powerful guiding forces. Cultivate gratitude for the abundance that still exists in your life, even amidst challenges. Focus on the resources, relationships, and strengths you possess, drawing upon them for support. Shift your perspective towards abundance by recognizing the abundance of opportunities, possibilities, and solutions available to you. By harnessing the power of gratitude and abundance, you gain a sense of resilience, inner strength, and the belief that you can overcome any adversity.

Summary
Overcoming challenges and cultivating resilience are integral parts of the journey towards manifesting with gratitude and abundance. When setbacks occur, maintaining gratitude allows us to find meaning, growth, and new opportunities within the difficulties. Building resilience and a positive mindset empowers us to face obstacles with strength and perseverance. And by utilizing gratitude and abundance as guiding forces, we navigate difficulties with grace and tap into the unlimited possibilities that await us. In the final section, we will explore ways to integrate gratitude and abundance into our everyday lives, deepening our connection with the flow of manifestations and creating a life of joy, fulfillment, and abundance.

Part 7: Cultivating a Gratitude and Abundance Lifestyle
As we near the end of our journey towards manifesting with gratitude and abundance, it is essential to shift from viewing gratitude and abundance as occasional practices to embracing them as a way of life. In this final section, we will explore how to integrate gratitude and abundance into our daily lives,

create a supportive environment, and sustain the practice for long-term manifestation. By cultivating a gratitude and abundance lifestyle, we open ourselves to the continuous flow of blessings and experiences that align with our desires.

A. Integrating Gratitude and Abundance into Daily Life
To make gratitude and abundance a part of our everyday lives, we must integrate them into our daily routines and activities. Begin each day with a gratitude practice, expressing appreciation for the blessings in your life. Throughout the day, consciously cultivate gratitude by finding moments of joy, beauty, and abundance in the present moment. Infuse your actions, interactions, and choices with a mindset of abundance, recognizing the limitless possibilities available to you. By weaving gratitude and abundance into the fabric of your daily life, you create a foundation for the manifestation of your desires.

B. Creating a Supportive Environment for Gratitude and Abundance
Our environment plays a significant role in sustaining a gratitude and abundance mindset. Surround yourself with positive influences, such as uplifting books, inspiring individuals, and supportive communities. Create physical spaces that reflect abundance, whether through symbols, affirmations, or visual representations of your desires. Cultivate relationships that uplift and encourage gratitude and abundance, sharing your journey with like-minded individuals who understand and support your aspirations. By consciously creating a supportive environment, you create fertile ground for the growth of gratitude and abundance in your life.

C. Sustaining the Practice of Gratitude and Abundance for Long-Term Manifestation
To sustain the practice of gratitude and abundance, consistency is key. Set reminders or create rituals to reinforce your gratitude practice throughout the day. Keep a gratitude journal where you can reflect on the blessings, manifestations, and growth you have experienced. Continuously reaffirm your commitment to gratitude and abundance through affirmations, visualizations, and acts of

kindness. Embrace the cyclical nature of manifestation, knowing that gratitude and abundance are an ongoing journey rather than a destination. By sustaining the practice over the long term, you strengthen your alignment with the flow of manifestations and deepen your connection with gratitude and abundance.

Summary
Cultivating a gratitude and abundance lifestyle is the culmination of our journey towards manifesting with joy and fulfillment. By integrating gratitude and abundance into our daily lives, we infuse every moment with appreciation and open ourselves to the limitless possibilities available to us. Creating a supportive environment ensures that gratitude and abundance thrive in our surroundings, while sustaining the practice over the long term strengthens our alignment with the flow of manifestations. As you embark on this lifestyle, remember that gratitude and abundance are transformative forces that invite miracles and blessings into your life. Embrace the power of gratitude and abundance, and allow them to guide you on your path to a life of joy, fulfillment, and limitless possibilities.

Conclusion: Cultivating Gratitude and Abundance

Congratulations on completing this enlightening journey towards cultivating gratitude and abundance! Throughout this chapter, we have explored the profound impact of gratitude and abundance on our mindset, well-being, and manifestation abilities. By embracing gratitude, practicing daily rituals, journaling, and navigating challenging situations with a mindset of abundance, you have laid a solid foundation for attracting and manifesting your desires.

Gratitude, the practice of appreciating and acknowledging the blessings in our lives, serves as a powerful catalyst for shifting our perspective and opening ourselves to abundance. It not only enhances our overall well-being but also aligns us with the abundant flow of the universe. By expressing gratitude for what we already have, we create a positive mindset that attracts more blessings into our lives.

In addition to gratitude, we have delved into the concept of abundance—recognizing and appreciating the abundance that surrounds us in various aspects of life. By shifting from a scarcity mindset to an abundance mindset, we invite abundance into every area of our lives, including relationships, opportunities, and experiences. Through affirmations, visualizations, and acts of kindness, we have learned to cultivate a sense of abundance that expands our possibilities and fuels our manifestations.

We have explored how gratitude and abundance extend beyond our personal lives and into our relationships with others. Nurturing gratitude in relationships strengthens the connections we have, while fostering a sense of abundance allows us to celebrate the successes and joys of others. By expressing gratitude and abundance through acts of kindness, we contribute to a positive cycle of giving and receiving, enhancing the overall abundance in our lives and the lives of those around us.

Manifesting with gratitude and abundance involves aligning our thoughts, emotions, and actions with the energy of gratitude and abundance. By setting intentions, aligning our focus and actions with gratitude and abundance, and surrendering to the flow of manifestations with trust, we become powerful creators of our reality. We learn to harness the innate power within us to bring our desires into physical manifestation.

Challenges are an inevitable part of our journey, but by maintaining gratitude in the face of setbacks, building resilience, and utilizing gratitude and abundance as guiding lights, we can overcome obstacles and continue our path of manifestation. By embracing a gratitude and abundance lifestyle, we integrate these principles into our daily lives, create a supportive environment, and sustain the practice for long-term manifestation.

Remember, the journey of cultivating gratitude and abundance is ongoing. It requires consistent practice, self-reflection, and a commitment to nurturing a positive mindset. As you continue this transformative path, may gratitude and abundance continue to guide you, opening the floodgates of manifestation and leading you to a life filled with joy, fulfillment, and limitless possibilities.

Embrace the power of gratitude and abundance, and watch as your life unfolds with blessings and manifestations beyond your wildest dreams. The keys to the floodgates of manifestation are in your hands. Now, go forth and create the abundant and fulfilling life you deserve!

Chapter 8: Creating Wealth and Prosperity: Abundance as Your Birthright

Welcome to the chapter on "Creating Wealth and Prosperity: Abundance as Your Birthright." In this chapter, we will explore the fascinating world of abundance and how it relates to your financial well-being.

Wealth and prosperity are essential aspects of a fulfilling and abundant life. While financial abundance is not the sole measure of success, it plays a significant role in creating opportunities, providing security, and enabling you to live the life you desire. Cultivating wealth and prosperity empowers you to pursue your dreams, support your loved ones, make a positive impact on society, and enjoy a sense of freedom and fulfillment.

In this chapter, we will delve into various aspects of wealth and prosperity, providing you with valuable insights and practical strategies to enhance your financial well-being. We will explore the concept of abundance and its relationship with mindset, as well as the importance of shifting your perspective from scarcity to abundance. You will discover powerful techniques to align your thoughts, emotions, and actions with wealth and prosperity, and learn how to attract abundance into your life using manifestation principles and the Law of Attraction.

Furthermore, we will discuss the significance of creating an environment that supports your wealth mindset, overcoming obstacles and building resilience on the path to abundance, and the transformative power of giving and sharing abundance with others. Lastly, we will explore the idea of sustaining long-term prosperity and finding a balance between material wealth and holistic well-being.

By the end of this chapter, you will have gained a deeper understanding of the principles and practices that can help you create wealth and prosperity in your life. So, let's embark on this enriching journey together and unlock the abundance that is your birthright.

Part 1: Understanding Abundance

To embark on the journey of creating wealth and prosperity, it is essential to understand the concept of abundance. Abundance goes beyond mere material possessions and encompasses a state of mind and being that allows for the flow of blessings and opportunities in various aspects of life. In this section, we will explore the meaning of abundance, its inherent connection to creating wealth and prosperity, and the role of mindset in experiencing abundance.

A. Definition and Concept of Abundance

Abundance can be defined as a state of plentifulness, where there is an ample supply of resources, opportunities, and positive experiences. It is the belief and recognition that there is enough for everyone to thrive and flourish. Abundance is not limited to financial wealth alone; it extends to all areas of life, including relationships, health, personal growth, and happiness. It is the understanding that the universe is abundant and inherently supportive of our well-being.

B. Recognizing Abundance as a Natural State

Abundance is not something external that needs to be acquired or attained; rather, it is our inherent birthright. Nature itself is abundant, with its vast array of flora, fauna, and resources. Just as there is an abundance of air to breathe and sunlight to nourish us, there is an abundance of opportunities and resources available to us in the world. Recognizing this inherent abundance helps us shift our perspective from scarcity to sufficiency and opens up our minds and hearts to the possibilities that lie ahead.

C. The Relationship Between Mindset and Abundance

Our mindset plays a crucial role in experiencing abundance and creating wealth and prosperity. The thoughts and beliefs we hold about ourselves, money, and the world around us shape our reality and influence our actions. A mindset rooted in abundance sees possibilities, embraces growth, and believes in the abundance of opportunities. Conversely, a scarcity mindset is characterized by fear, limitation, and a belief in lack. By cultivating a mindset of abundance, we open ourselves up to receive and attract wealth and prosperity into our lives.

Summary

Understanding abundance is a fundamental aspect of creating wealth and prosperity. It involves recognizing the inherent abundance that exists in the world, shifting our mindset from scarcity to sufficiency, and embracing the belief that we are deserving of abundance in all its forms. As we continue our exploration, we will delve deeper into the principles and practices that will enable us to tap into this natural state of abundance and manifest wealth and prosperity in our lives.

Part 2: Shifting Your Mindset

Shifting our mindset is a crucial step in creating wealth and prosperity. Our thoughts and beliefs shape our reality, and by identifying and overcoming a scarcity mindset, we can cultivate a mindset of abundance and possibility. In this section, we will explore practical strategies to shift our mindset, harness the power of positive affirmations and self-talk, and embrace an abundant perspective that paves the way for creating wealth and prosperity.

A. Identifying and Overcoming Scarcity Mindset

The first step in shifting our mindset is to identify and overcome any scarcity mindset that may be holding us back. A scarcity mindset is characterized by a belief in lack, limitation, and a fear of not having enough. It often manifests as negative thoughts and self-doubt, which hinder our ability to see and seize opportunities. By becoming aware of these patterns and challenging them, we can break free from the grip of scarcity and open ourselves to abundance.

B. Cultivating a Mindset of Abundance and Possibility
Cultivating a mindset of abundance involves embracing the belief that there is an abundance of opportunities, resources, and wealth available to us. It requires shifting our focus from what we lack to what we have and can create. This mindset encourages us to adopt a growth-oriented perspective, where challenges are seen as opportunities for growth and learning. By cultivating a mindset of possibility, we expand our vision, unleash our creativity, and attract wealth and prosperity into our lives.

C. The Power of Positive Affirmations and Self-Talk
Positive affirmations and self-talk play a vital role in shaping our mindset and creating a positive mental environment. Affirmations are positive statements that affirm our desired reality, and when repeated regularly, they help rewire our subconscious mind to align with abundance. By consciously choosing empowering affirmations and incorporating them into our daily routine, we reinforce positive beliefs, dissolve limiting beliefs, and strengthen our belief in our ability to create wealth and prosperity. Our self-talk, the ongoing internal dialogue we have with ourselves, also influences our mindset. By replacing negative self-talk with encouraging and supportive language, we can nurture an empowering mindset that propels us towards abundance.

Summary
Shifting our mindset is a transformative process that lays the foundation for creating wealth and prosperity. By identifying and overcoming scarcity mindset, cultivating a mindset of abundance and possibility, and harnessing the power of positive affirmations and self-talk, we can rewire our thoughts and beliefs to align with abundance. As we continue on this journey, we will explore further strategies and practices that will support us in embracing an abundant mindset and manifesting wealth and prosperity in our lives.

Part 3: Embracing Abundance Consciousness
Embracing abundance consciousness is an essential aspect of creating wealth and prosperity. It involves shifting our awareness and mindset to recognize and appreciate the abundance that already exists in our lives. In this section, we

will explore practices and principles that will help us cultivate gratitude for existing abundance, expand our perception of abundance in all areas of life, and develop a sense of deservingness and worthiness, all of which are vital for creating wealth and prosperity.

A. Cultivating Gratitude for Existing Abundance

Gratitude is a powerful practice that allows us to acknowledge and appreciate the abundance that surrounds us. By cultivating gratitude, we shift our focus from what we lack to what we have, nurturing a positive and abundant mindset. Taking time each day to express gratitude for the blessings, resources, and opportunities we already possess creates a ripple effect of attracting more abundance into our lives. Gratitude acts as a magnet, drawing in more reasons to be grateful and creating a fertile ground for creating wealth and prosperity.

B. Expanding the Perception of Abundance in All Areas of Life

Expanding our perception of abundance involves recognizing that abundance is not limited to financial wealth alone. It encompasses all aspects of our lives, including health, relationships, personal growth, and experiences. By consciously shifting our attention to the abundance present in these areas, we open ourselves up to receiving more blessings and opportunities. Developing an expansive mindset that embraces abundance in all its forms allows us to tap into the infinite possibilities that exist and align with the flow of creating wealth and prosperity.

C. Developing a Sense of Deservingness and Worthiness

A crucial aspect of embracing abundance consciousness is developing a deep sense of deservingness and worthiness. Often, subconscious beliefs rooted in scarcity can undermine our ability to receive and manifest abundance. By recognizing our inherent worthiness and releasing any self-limiting beliefs, we open ourselves up to receiving the abundance that is our birthright. Developing self-love, self-acceptance, and self-worth are essential steps in creating a strong foundation for attracting and creating wealth and prosperity.

Summary
Embracing abundance consciousness is a transformative
journey that requires us to cultivate gratitude for existing
abundance, expand our perception of abundance in all areas
of life, and develop a sense of deservingness and worthiness.
By embracing the abundance that already surrounds us,
shifting our mindset, and aligning our beliefs with the flow of
abundance, we set the stage for creating wealth and
prosperity. As we continue on this path, we will explore
further practices and principles that will support us in
manifesting our desires and experiencing the fullness of
abundance in our lives.

Part 4: Aligning Actions with Abundance

Aligning our actions with abundance is a vital step in creating
wealth and prosperity. It involves setting clear goals and
intentions, taking inspired action, and overcoming fear to
embrace calculated risks. In this section, we will explore
practical strategies that will help us align our actions with the
abundance we seek, ensuring that we are moving in the
direction of creating wealth and prosperity.

A. Setting Clear Goals and Intentions for Wealth and Prosperity

To align our actions with abundance, it is crucial to set clear
goals and intentions. Clearly defining what we desire to
achieve in terms of wealth and prosperity allows us to create a
roadmap for success. By setting specific, measurable,
achievable, relevant, and time-bound (SMART) goals, we
provide ourselves with a clear direction and purpose. These
goals act as a compass, guiding our actions and decisions
towards the manifestation of wealth and prosperity.

B. Taking Inspired Action Towards Abundance

Once we have set clear goals and intentions, it is essential to
take inspired action. Inspired action refers to taking steps
that are aligned with our desires and values, guided by our
intuition and inner wisdom. Rather than simply going
through the motions, inspired action is driven by passion,
purpose, and enthusiasm. It is about taking deliberate and
focused steps that propel us forward on the path of creating
wealth and prosperity. When we align our actions with our

desires, we tap into the energy of abundance and open ourselves up to opportunities that will support our journey.

C. Overcoming Fear and Embracing Calculated Risks

Fear can often hold us back from taking the necessary actions to create wealth and prosperity. However, to align with abundance, we must learn to overcome fear and embrace calculated risks. It is essential to recognize that growth and success often require stepping outside of our comfort zones and taking risks. By reframing our perspective on fear and understanding that it is a natural part of the process, we can approach risks with a calculated mindset. This involves evaluating potential risks and rewards, gathering information, and making informed decisions. Embracing calculated risks allows us to expand our possibilities and create opportunities for wealth and prosperity.

Summary

Aligning our actions with abundance is a powerful way to create wealth and prosperity in our lives. By setting clear goals and intentions, taking inspired action, and overcoming fear to embrace calculated risks, we position ourselves on the path of abundance. As we align our actions with our desires and values, we tap into the flow of abundance and open ourselves up to the opportunities and resources necessary for creating wealth and prosperity. In the next section, we will explore further strategies that will support us in manifesting our goals and experiencing the fullness of abundance in our lives.

Part 5: Attracting Wealth and Prosperity

Attracting wealth and prosperity is a powerful practice that can help us manifest the abundant life we desire. By utilizing visualization and manifestation techniques, harnessing the power of the Law of Attraction, and integrating abundance rituals and daily habits into our lives, we can align ourselves with the flow of abundance and create the conditions for creating wealth and prosperity.

A. Utilizing Visualization and Manifestation Techniques

Visualization and manifestation techniques are effective tools for attracting wealth and prosperity. By creating vivid mental images of the abundance we desire, we tap into the power of our imagination and send a clear message to the universe about our intentions. Visualization allows us to align our thoughts, emotions, and energy with the frequency of abundance, making it easier for us to attract the wealth and prosperity we seek. Combined with focused intention and belief, visualization becomes a potent practice for manifesting our desires.

B. Harnessing the Power of the Law of Attraction

The Law of Attraction states that like attracts like. By focusing our thoughts, emotions, and beliefs on wealth and prosperity, we can magnetize these experiences into our lives. The Law of Attraction emphasizes the importance of aligning our internal state with our desired external reality. By cultivating a positive mindset, practicing gratitude, and affirming our abundance, we raise our vibration and attract more wealth and prosperity into our experience. Understanding and applying the principles of the Law of Attraction can significantly enhance our ability to create wealth and prosperity.

C. Practicing Abundance Rituals and Daily Habits

Practicing abundance rituals and incorporating daily habits that support our wealth and prosperity goals can create a powerful momentum towards creating the life of abundance we desire. Abundance rituals can vary from person to person, but they often involve activities such as journaling, affirmations, meditation, and visualization specific to attracting wealth and prosperity. Additionally, integrating daily habits such as gratitude practice, positive affirmations, and consciously choosing thoughts and actions aligned with abundance reinforces our commitment to creating wealth and prosperity in our lives.

Summary

Attracting wealth and prosperity is a deliberate and intentional practice that requires us to utilize visualization and manifestation techniques, harness the power of the Law of Attraction, and integrate abundance rituals and daily habits into our lives. By aligning our thoughts, emotions, and actions with the frequency of abundance, we open ourselves up to the unlimited possibilities and opportunities that exist for creating wealth and prosperity. In the next section, we will explore additional strategies that will support us in creating a prosperous mindset and overcoming any limiting beliefs that may hinder our journey towards abundance.

Part 6: Creating a Wealth-Mindset Environment

Creating a wealth-mindset environment is crucial for supporting our journey towards creating wealth and prosperity. By surrounding ourselves with positive influences and like-minded individuals, creating an environment that supports wealth and prosperity, and letting go of negative influences and limiting beliefs, we can create a powerful ecosystem that nurtures our wealth mindset and propels us towards achieving our financial goals.

A. Surrounding Yourself with Positive Influences and Like-Minded Individuals

Surrounding ourselves with positive influences and like-minded individuals is essential for fostering a wealth mindset. By associating with people who share similar goals and aspirations, we can draw inspiration, support, and valuable insights from their experiences. Positive influences can include mentors, coaches, or successful individuals who have already achieved the level of wealth and prosperity we aspire to. Their wisdom and guidance can provide us with valuable strategies, mindset shifts, and motivation to overcome challenges and stay focused on our journey of creating wealth and prosperity.

B. Creating an Environment that Supports Wealth and Prosperity

Our environment plays a significant role in shaping our beliefs, habits, and actions. Creating an environment that supports wealth and prosperity involves optimizing our physical space, such as our home or workspace, to reflect abundance and success. This can include organizing our space in a way that promotes productivity, decluttering to create a sense of order and clarity, and incorporating visual cues that symbolize wealth and prosperity, such as inspiring quotes, vision boards, or abundance affirmations. By consciously designing our environment to align with our wealth goals, we create a constant reminder and reinforcement of our commitment to creating wealth and prosperity.

C. Letting Go of Negative Influences and Limiting Beliefs
To truly create a wealth-mindset environment, it is crucial to identify and let go of negative influences and limiting beliefs that may be holding us back. Negative influences can come in the form of toxic relationships, pessimistic attitudes, or self-doubt. These influences drain our energy and hinder our progress towards wealth and prosperity. Similarly, limiting beliefs such as "money is scarce" or "I am not deserving of wealth" create mental barriers that prevent us from taking the necessary actions for financial success. By actively challenging and replacing these negative influences and limiting beliefs with empowering ones, we create space for abundance to flow into our lives.

Summary
Creating a wealth-mindset environment is a powerful step towards creating wealth and prosperity. By surrounding ourselves with positive influences and like-minded individuals, creating an environment that supports our financial goals, and letting go of negative influences and limiting beliefs, we set ourselves up for success. Our environment has a profound impact on our thoughts, emotions, and actions, and by consciously designing it to align with abundance, we create a fertile ground for creating wealth and prosperity. In the next section, we will explore practical strategies for taking inspired actions and implementing effective wealth-building techniques to manifest our financial goals.

Part 7: Overcoming Obstacles on the Path to Abundance
The journey to creating wealth and prosperity is not without its challenges. However, it is through overcoming these obstacles that we grow, learn, and ultimately manifest our desired abundance. In this section, we will explore strategies for dealing with setbacks and challenges, building resilience, maintaining a positive attitude, and seeking support from mentors or coaches on our path to creating wealth and prosperity.

A. Dealing with Setbacks and Challenges

Setbacks and challenges are inevitable on the path to abundance. Whether it's financial setbacks, unexpected expenses, or market fluctuations, it's important to approach them with resilience and a problem-solving mindset. Instead of allowing setbacks to discourage us, we can view them as opportunities for growth and learning. By analyzing the situation, identifying potential solutions, and taking decisive action, we can navigate through challenges and continue moving forward on our journey towards creating wealth and prosperity.

B. Building Resilience and Maintaining a Positive Attitude

Building resilience is essential for overcoming obstacles and maintaining a positive attitude in the face of adversity. Resilience allows us to bounce back from setbacks, adapt to changing circumstances, and stay focused on our goals. Cultivating a positive attitude involves reframing challenges as opportunities, practicing gratitude for the lessons learned, and staying optimistic about the possibilities of creating wealth and prosperity. By nurturing resilience and maintaining a positive mindset, we develop the mental strength and perseverance necessary to overcome obstacles on our path to abundance.

C. Seeking Support and Learning from Mentors or Coaches

Seeking support from mentors or coaches can be immensely valuable on our journey towards creating wealth and prosperity. Mentors and coaches provide guidance, wisdom, and a fresh perspective based on their own experiences and expertise. They can help us navigate challenges, offer insights and strategies, and hold us accountable to our goals. Learning from those who have already achieved the level of success we aspire to can provide us with valuable insights, shortcuts, and inspiration. By seeking support and learning from mentors or coaches, we accelerate our progress and increase our chances of creating lasting wealth and prosperity.

Summary

Overcoming obstacles on the path to abundance is an integral part of our journey towards creating wealth and prosperity. By effectively dealing with setbacks and challenges, building resilience, maintaining a positive attitude, and seeking support from mentors or coaches, we can overcome obstacles with determination and grace. The lessons learned from these experiences not only strengthen our character but also deepen our understanding of the principles and strategies for creating lasting wealth and prosperity. In the next section, we will delve into practical steps for sustaining our wealth-mindset and integrating abundance into our daily lives for long-term manifestation.

Part 8: Giving and Sharing Abundance

As we journey towards creating wealth and prosperity, it is essential to recognize the profound impact of giving and sharing abundance. In this section, we will explore the significance of generosity in attracting wealth, the power of contributing to causes and communities, and the ripple effect of abundance created through giving. By embracing the spirit of giving, we not only uplift others but also open ourselves up to receiving even greater abundance in return.

A. The Significance of Generosity in Attracting Wealth

Generosity plays a vital role in attracting wealth and creating a prosperous mindset. When we give freely, whether it's our time, resources, or knowledge, we demonstrate an abundance mentality. By shifting our focus from scarcity to abundance, we align ourselves with the flow of abundance in the universe. The act of giving sends a powerful message to the universe that we are open and receptive to receiving more. As we give generously, we create a positive energy exchange and establish a harmonious relationship with wealth and prosperity.

B. Contributing to Causes and Communities

Contributing to causes and communities is a meaningful way to share our abundance and make a positive impact in the world. By identifying causes that resonate with our values and passions, we can channel our resources towards creating positive change. Whether it's supporting educational initiatives, environmental conservation, or social welfare programs, our contributions have the potential to transform lives and uplift communities. Additionally, active involvement in community initiatives allows us to expand our network, build meaningful connections, and open doors to new opportunities for creating wealth and prosperity.

C. Creating a Ripple Effect of Abundance Through Giving

Giving has a powerful ripple effect that extends far beyond the immediate impact. When we give freely and share our abundance, we inspire others to do the same. Our acts of generosity serve as a catalyst for creating a culture of abundance, where giving becomes a natural and reciprocal phenomenon. As we contribute to the growth and success of others, we create an energetic flow of abundance that expands exponentially. This ripple effect not only enriches the lives of individuals but also contributes to the collective well-being and prosperity of society as a whole.

Summary

Giving and sharing abundance is a transformative practice that holds immense significance on our journey towards creating wealth and prosperity. By embracing generosity, we align ourselves with the flow of abundance, attract greater wealth into our lives, and create a positive impact in the world. Through contributing to causes and communities, we leverage our resources to make a difference and open doors to new opportunities. Furthermore, the ripple effect of abundance created through our acts of giving expands the circle of prosperity, benefiting both individuals and society as a whole. In the final section, we will explore the culmination of our efforts and delve into the art of consciously manifesting wealth and prosperity in all aspects of our lives.

Part 9: Sustaining Long-Term Prosperity

As we near the end of our journey towards creating wealth and prosperity, it is crucial to explore the keys to sustaining long-term abundance. In this section, we will delve into the importance of cultivating a wealth consciousness as a lifelong practice, continuously expanding and evolving our definition of abundance, and striking a balance between material wealth and holistic well-being. By integrating these principles into our lives, we lay the foundation for lasting prosperity and fulfillment.

A. Cultivating a Wealth Consciousness as a Lifelong Practice
Creating wealth and prosperity is not a one-time event but an ongoing journey. It requires cultivating a wealth consciousness that becomes an integral part of our daily lives. This practice involves consistently aligning our thoughts, beliefs, and actions with abundance. By nurturing a mindset of abundance, we train our minds to recognize and attract opportunities for creating wealth and prosperity. It involves embracing positive affirmations, visualization techniques, and regular self-reflection to reinforce our wealth consciousness and maintain a state of abundance.

B. Continuously Expanding and Evolving Your Definition of Abundance
To sustain long-term prosperity, it is essential to continuously expand and evolve our definition of abundance. True abundance encompasses more than just material wealth. It includes aspects such as meaningful relationships, personal growth, health, and happiness. By broadening our perspective, we tap into the richness of life beyond monetary gains. This expansion allows us to appreciate the diverse forms of abundance that exist and opens doors to new possibilities for creating wealth and prosperity in various areas of our lives.

C. Balancing Material Wealth with Holistic Well-Being
While material wealth is an important aspect of creating prosperity, it is equally vital to balance it with holistic well-being. Sustaining long-term prosperity requires nurturing our physical, mental, and emotional well-being. This entails prioritizing self-care, maintaining healthy relationships, and pursuing passions and hobbies that bring fulfillment. By finding harmony between material wealth and holistic well-being, we create a foundation for sustained success and lasting happiness.

Summary
Sustaining long-term prosperity is a continuous journey that requires a conscious and committed approach. By cultivating a wealth consciousness as a lifelong practice, we align ourselves with the flow of abundance and attract ongoing opportunities for creating wealth and prosperity.

Continuously expanding our definition of abundance allows us to appreciate and embrace the multifaceted aspects of a prosperous life. Moreover, striking a balance between material wealth and holistic well-being ensures that our journey towards prosperity is fulfilling and sustainable. As we conclude this chapter, let us carry forward the knowledge and practices we have learned, embracing the abundant possibilities that lie ahead in our pursuit of creating wealth and prosperity.

Conclusion: Creating Wealth and Prosperity

Congratulations on completing the journey of exploring wealth and prosperity, understanding abundance as your birthright. Throughout this chapter, we have delved into various aspects of creating wealth and prosperity, from understanding abundance to shifting our mindset, embracing abundance consciousness, aligning actions, attracting wealth, creating a wealth-mindset environment, overcoming obstacles, giving and sharing abundance, and sustaining long-term prosperity.

We have learned that abundance is not limited to material wealth alone but encompasses a holistic and abundant life in all its facets. By adopting a mindset of abundance and aligning our thoughts, beliefs, and actions with wealth and prosperity, we open ourselves up to unlimited possibilities and opportunities. It is through this intentional alignment that we can manifest and create the life of abundance we desire.

Remember, creating wealth and prosperity is an ongoing journey that requires dedication, self-reflection, and continuous growth. By nurturing a wealth consciousness and expanding our definition of abundance, we unlock new levels of fulfillment and purpose. It is important to cultivate an environment that supports our aspirations and surround ourselves with positive influences and like-minded individuals who uplift and inspire us on our path.

Inevitably, we may encounter setbacks and obstacles along the way. However, by maintaining a positive attitude, building resilience, seeking support, and learning from mentors or coaches, we can navigate these challenges and emerge stronger and more determined.

Furthermore, generosity and giving play a crucial role in attracting wealth and prosperity. By contributing to causes and communities, we create a ripple effect of abundance, fostering a cycle of giving and receiving that benefits not only ourselves but also those around us.

Lastly, sustaining long-term prosperity involves balancing material wealth with holistic well-being. This requires taking care of our physical, mental, and emotional health, nurturing meaningful relationships, and finding fulfillment beyond monetary gains. By integrating these elements into our lives, we create a solid foundation for sustained success and lasting happiness.

As we conclude this chapter, I encourage you to continue exploring and expanding your understanding of wealth and prosperity. Embrace the abundance that is your birthright and remember that creating wealth is not a selfish pursuit but a means to positively impact your own life and the lives of others. Stay committed to your journey, practice gratitude, and keep aligning your thoughts, beliefs, and actions with abundance. With the right mindset, habits, and actions, you have the power to create the abundant life you desire.

Wishing you abundant success, fulfillment, and prosperity on your remarkable journey of creating wealth and prosperity.

Chapter 9: Manifesting Health and Well-Being: Nurturing Your Body, Mind, and Spirit

Welcome to the chapter on "Manifesting Health and Well-being: Nurturing Your Body, Mind, and Spirit." In this chapter, we will explore the vital aspects of our well-being and how we can nurture ourselves holistically to lead a healthy and fulfilling life.

Health and well-being are the cornerstones of a balanced and satisfying life. They provide the foundation for us to thrive physically, mentally, and emotionally. When we prioritize our well-being, we can experience increased vitality, inner peace, and a greater sense of fulfillment.

Throughout this chapter, we will delve into various aspects of health and well-being, examining the interconnection between our body, mind, and spirit. We will discuss practical strategies and insights to help you nurture and manifest a state of optimal well-being in your life. From understanding the holistic nature of health to exploring self-care practices and embracing spiritual well-being, we will cover a range of topics designed to support your journey towards vibrant health and fulfillment.

So, let's embark on this enlightening exploration of *Manifesting Health and Well-Being*, as we discover how to nurture our body, mind, and spirit for a balanced and thriving life.

Part 1: Understanding Health and Well-Being

In this section, we will explore the fundamental aspects of health and well-being, emphasizing their holistic nature and the importance of self-care and self-awareness in manifesting optimal well-being in our lives. Understanding these concepts will empower us to take charge of our health and nurture our body, mind, and spirit.

A. Definition and Holistic Nature of Health and Well-Being

Health and well-being encompass more than just the absence of illness; they represent a state of complete physical, mental, and social well-being. It involves finding a balance in various aspects of our lives, including our physical health, emotional well-being, social connections, and spiritual alignment. *Manifesting Health and Well-Being* requires us to consider the whole person, recognizing the interconnectedness of different aspects of our being.

B. Recognizing the Interconnectedness of the Body, Mind, and Spirit

Our well-being is not limited to the physical realm but is deeply intertwined with our mental and spiritual aspects. The body, mind, and spirit are interconnected, each influencing and impacting the others. When we manifest health and well-being, we nurture these interconnected aspects, acknowledging that a healthy body supports a healthy mind and spirit, and vice versa. It is through this interconnectedness that we can achieve a state of holistic well-being.

C. The Significance of Self-Care and Self-Awareness

Self-care and self-awareness play crucial roles in *Manifesting Health and Well-Being*. Self-care involves making intentional choices that prioritize our physical, emotional, and spiritual needs. It encompasses activities that nourish and support our well-being, such as proper nutrition, exercise, restful sleep, stress management, and engaging in activities that bring joy and fulfillment. Self-awareness involves cultivating a deep understanding of ourselves, our emotions, thoughts, and beliefs, allowing us to make conscious choices that align with our well-being. By practicing self-care and self-awareness, we create a solid foundation for manifesting optimal health and well-being.

Summary

Understanding health and well-being is the first step towards manifesting a vibrant and fulfilling life. By embracing the holistic nature of these concepts, recognizing the interconnectedness of our body, mind, and spirit, and prioritizing self-care and self-awareness, we lay the groundwork for nurturing our well-being. In the upcoming sections, we will delve deeper into specific strategies and practices that will empower us to manifest health and well-being in our everyday lives. So, let's continue our journey towards *Manifesting Health and Well-Being* by exploring the interconnected aspects of our being.

Part 2: Nurturing Your Physical Health

In this section, we will explore the essential practices for nurturing your physical health as a key component of manifesting overall health and well-being. Taking care of your physical well-being provides a solid foundation for a thriving life. By adopting healthy habits and making conscious choices, you can manifest vibrant health and enhance your overall well-being.

A. Maintaining a Balanced and Nutritious Diet

A balanced and nutritious diet is vital for *Manifesting Health and Well-Being*. It involves nourishing your body with a variety of whole foods that provide essential nutrients, vitamins, and minerals. Focus on incorporating a colorful array of fruits, vegetables, whole grains, lean proteins, and healthy fats into your meals. Be mindful of portion sizes and practice moderation to maintain a balanced diet. By nourishing your body with the right foods, you support its optimal functioning and manifest vibrant health.

B. Regular Physical Exercise and Its Benefits

Regular physical exercise is a powerful tool for *Manifesting Health and Well-Being*. Engaging in physical activity not only improves your physical fitness but also positively impacts your mental and emotional well-being. Find activities that you enjoy, whether it's walking, jogging, dancing, swimming, or practicing yoga. Aim for at least 150 minutes of moderate-intensity aerobic exercise per week, along with strength-training exercises. Exercise boosts your energy, strengthens your immune system, improves your mood, and promotes overall wellness.

C. Getting Enough Sleep and Managing Stress Levels

Adequate sleep and stress management are essential for *Manifesting Health and Well-Being*. Sleep plays a vital role in the body's restoration and rejuvenation processes. Aim for 7-9 hours of quality sleep each night, establishing a consistent sleep routine and creating a sleep-friendly environment. Additionally, managing stress levels is crucial as chronic stress can have detrimental effects on your health. Practice stress management techniques such as deep breathing, meditation, mindfulness, and engaging in activities that bring you joy and relaxation. By prioritizing sleep and managing stress, you support your body's natural healing and manifest optimal well-being.

Summary
Nurturing your physical health is a key aspect of manifesting overall health and well-being. By maintaining a balanced and nutritious diet, engaging in regular physical exercise, and prioritizing adequate sleep and stress management, you lay a solid foundation for vibrant health. These practices not only benefit your physical well-being but also positively impact your mental and emotional state. Embrace these habits as part of your lifestyle and witness the transformative power they have in *Manifesting Health and Well-Being*. In the upcoming sections, we will delve deeper into nurturing the mind and spirit to create a holistic approach to manifesting optimal well-being. So, let's continue our journey towards *Manifesting Health and Well-Being* by exploring the interconnected aspects of our being.

Part 3: Cultivating Mental and Emotional Well-Being

In this section, we will explore the essential practices for cultivating mental and emotional well-being, which are integral to manifesting overall health and well-being. Our thoughts, emotions, and mindset greatly influence our overall state of being. By nurturing our mental and emotional well-being, we can manifest a sense of inner peace, resilience, and overall happiness.

A. Developing Positive Thought Patterns and Mindset

Developing positive thought patterns and cultivating a positive mindset is vital for *Manifesting Health and Well-Being*. Our thoughts shape our reality and influence our emotions. Practice self-awareness and consciously choose to focus on positive aspects of your life and the world around you. Replace negative self-talk and limiting beliefs with affirmations and empowering thoughts. By consciously shifting your thought patterns and embracing a positive mindset, you create a foundation for manifesting mental and emotional well-being.

B. Practicing Mindfulness and Stress Reduction Techniques
Mindfulness and stress reduction techniques are powerful tools for *Manifesting Health and Well-Being*. Mindfulness involves bringing your attention to the present moment without judgment. Engage in practices such as meditation, deep breathing exercises, and yoga to cultivate mindfulness. These practices help reduce stress, enhance self-awareness, and promote emotional well-being. Take time each day to slow down, connect with your breath, and engage in activities that bring you peace and joy.

C. Building Resilience and Managing Emotions Effectively
Building resilience and managing emotions effectively are essential for *Manifesting Health and Well-Being*. Life presents us with challenges and setbacks, but our ability to bounce back and adapt is crucial. Cultivate resilience by nurturing a positive mindset, seeking support from loved ones, and practicing self-care. Additionally, develop emotional intelligence by acknowledging and accepting your emotions, finding healthy outlets for expression, and learning effective coping strategies. By building resilience and managing emotions, you manifest emotional well-being and enhance your overall mental health.

Summary
Cultivating mental and emotional well-being is a vital aspect of manifesting overall health and well-being. By developing positive thought patterns and mindset, practicing mindfulness and stress reduction techniques, and building resilience and managing emotions effectively, you create a strong foundation for inner peace, happiness, and resilience. These practices empower you to navigate life's challenges with grace and manifest a state of well-being. As we continue our journey towards *Manifesting Health and Well-Being*, let us explore the next section, which focuses on nurturing the spirit and connecting with a higher purpose. So, let's dive

deeper into the interconnected aspects of our being and continue *Manifesting Health and Well-Being* in our lives.

Part 4: Enhancing Spiritual Well-Being
In this section, we will delve into the realm of spiritual well-being and its significant role in manifesting overall health and well-being. Spiritual well-being encompasses our connection with something greater than ourselves, a sense of purpose, and finding meaning in life. By nurturing our spiritual aspect, we can tap into a profound source of inner strength, peace, and fulfillment.

A. Exploring Spirituality and Its Role in Overall Well-Being
Spirituality refers to our connection with the sacred, higher power, or the deeper aspects of life. It is a personal and subjective experience that varies for each individual. Exploring spirituality allows us to transcend the material realm and discover a sense of interconnectedness and purpose. Spiritual well-being complements physical and mental well-being, contributing to our overall health. It provides solace during challenging times, fosters a sense of hope, and allows us to find meaning and purpose in our lives.

B. Engaging in Spiritual Practices and Rituals
Engaging in spiritual practices and rituals is a powerful way to nurture our spiritual well-being. These practices can include meditation, prayer, contemplation, journaling, or engaging in nature walks. Such activities help us connect with our inner selves, cultivate mindfulness, and deepen our spiritual awareness. By incorporating spiritual practices into our daily lives, we create sacred spaces and moments that nurture our souls and contribute to our overall well-being.

C. Finding Meaning and Purpose in Life
Finding meaning and purpose in life is a crucial aspect of *Manifesting Health and Well-Being*. It involves aligning our actions and values with a higher purpose and living in accordance with our authentic selves. Reflect on your passions, values, and what brings you joy and fulfillment. Seek activities and relationships that align with your purpose

and contribute to the well-being of others. By living a life of meaning and purpose, you foster a deep sense of fulfillment, contentment, and spiritual well-being.

Summary
Enhancing spiritual well-being is an integral part of manifesting overall health and well-being. Exploring spirituality, engaging in spiritual practices and rituals, and finding meaning and purpose in life contribute to our inner growth, peace, and connection with the sacred. By nurturing our spiritual aspect, we tap into a profound source of strength and find solace and guidance during life's challenges. As we continue our journey towards *Manifesting Health and Well-Being*, let us now delve into the final section, which focuses on fostering harmonious relationships and social well-being. So, let's explore the power of connections and continue *Manifesting Health and Well-Being* in our lives.

Part 5: Creating a Healthy Lifestyle

In this section, we will explore the importance of creating a healthy lifestyle and how it contributes to manifesting overall health and well-being. A healthy lifestyle involves incorporating beneficial habits into our daily routines, cultivating supportive relationships and social connections, and creating a nurturing living environment. By consciously adopting these practices, we empower ourselves to live a life filled with vitality, balance, and well-being.

A. Incorporating Healthy Habits into Daily Routines

Incorporating healthy habits into our daily routines is essential for manifesting and maintaining optimal health and well-being. This includes practices such as eating a balanced diet, staying hydrated, engaging in regular physical exercise, and prioritizing rest and relaxation. By making conscious choices to nourish our bodies with nutritious food, move regularly, and give ourselves adequate rest, we support our physical, mental, and emotional well-being. These habits serve as the foundation for a healthy lifestyle, allowing us to thrive and manifest health and well-being in our lives.

B. Building Supportive Relationships and Social Connections

Building supportive relationships and fostering social connections is a fundamental aspect of *Manifesting Health and Well-Being*. Humans are social beings, and meaningful connections with others contribute to our overall sense of happiness and fulfillment. Cultivating relationships that are supportive, uplifting, and nurturing helps us navigate life's challenges, provides emotional support, and promotes a sense of belonging. Engaging in activities and groups that align with our interests and values allows us to connect with like-minded individuals, creating a supportive network that enhances our well-being.

C. Creating a Nurturing and Harmonious Living Environment

Creating a nurturing and harmonious living environment is vital for our well-being. Our physical surroundings greatly influence our mood, energy levels, and overall state of being. By organizing and decluttering our living spaces, we create a sense of order and tranquility. Incorporating elements that promote relaxation and rejuvenation, such as plants, natural light, and calming colors, can positively impact our well-being. It is also important to establish healthy boundaries, maintain a clean and safe environment, and surround ourselves with positive influences that align with our values and aspirations.

Summary

Creating a healthy lifestyle is a key component of *Manifesting Health and Well-Being* in our lives. By incorporating healthy habits into our daily routines, building supportive relationships and social connections, and creating a nurturing living environment, we cultivate a foundation for optimal well-being. These practices empower us to lead fulfilling lives filled with vitality, balance, and a deep sense of well-being. As we conclude our exploration of *Manifesting Health and Well-Being*, let us now move forward to the final section, which focuses on the power of gratitude and cultivating a positive mindset. So, let's dive into the transformative practices that allow us to embrace gratitude and nurture our minds for *Manifesting Health and Well-Being*.

Part 6: Holistic Approaches to Well-Being

In our quest to manifest health and well-being, it is essential to explore holistic approaches that address our physical, mental, and spiritual aspects. Holistic practices recognize the interconnectedness of our being and aim to promote overall well-being. In this section, we will delve into alternative therapies, mind-body practices, and sustainable living practices that contribute to *Manifesting Health and Well-Being* in a comprehensive way.

A. Exploring Alternative Therapies and Complementary Modalities

Alternative therapies and complementary modalities offer additional avenues for enhancing our well-being. These practices, which go beyond conventional medicine, focus on restoring balance and promoting the body's natural healing mechanisms. Examples include acupuncture, aromatherapy, herbal medicine, and energy healing modalities like Reiki. By exploring these therapies, we can discover new ways to support our well-being and manifest health on multiple levels.

B. Integrating Mind-Body Practices Such as Yoga and Meditation

Mind-body practices such as yoga and meditation are powerful tools for cultivating balance, inner peace, and well-being. Yoga combines physical postures, breathing exercises, and meditation to promote strength, flexibility, and relaxation. Meditation, on the other hand, trains our minds to focus, cultivate mindfulness, and reduce stress. By integrating these practices into our lives, we can enhance our mind-body connection, improve mental clarity, reduce anxiety, and nurture a sense of overall well-being.

C. Embracing Natural and Sustainable Living Practices

Embracing natural and sustainable living practices is not only beneficial for our individual well-being but also for the well-being of the planet. Choosing organic and locally sourced foods, reducing our carbon footprint, and opting for eco-friendly products contribute to our overall health and the health of the environment. Connecting with nature, spending time outdoors, and practicing environmental stewardship can bring about a sense of harmony and well-being. By aligning our actions with sustainable living practices, we create a positive impact on ourselves and the world around us.

Summary
Holistic approaches to well-being encompass a wide range of practices that address our physical, mental, and spiritual aspects. Exploring alternative therapies and complementary modalities allows us to discover new avenues for supporting our well-being. Integrating mind-body practices such as yoga and meditation strengthens our connection between the body and mind, promoting inner balance and peace. Embracing natural and sustainable living practices nurtures both our well-being and the well-being of the planet. By embracing these holistic approaches, we align ourselves with the principles of *Manifesting Health and Well-Being* in a comprehensive and interconnected manner. As we conclude this section, let us move forward to the final part of our journey, where we explore the power of gratitude and its transformative effects on *Manifesting Health and Well-Being*.

Part 7: Manifesting Health and Well-Being

Manifesting Health and Well-Being is not merely about physical fitness or absence of illness; it involves nurturing all aspects of our being to achieve a state of optimal well-being. In this section, we will explore powerful techniques and practices that support the manifestation of health and well-being. By setting intentions, utilizing visualization and manifestation techniques, and embracing gratitude and self-love, we can actively participate in our own well-being and create a life of vitality and balance.

A. Setting Intentions for Optimal Health and Well-Being

Setting clear intentions is a powerful first step in *Manifesting Health and Well-Being*. By defining what we desire and envisioning our ideal state of well-being, we create a focused direction for our journey. Intentions serve as a guidepost, reminding us of our goals and motivating us to take action. Whether it is to cultivate mental clarity, boost physical vitality, or nurture emotional balance, setting intentions allows us to align our thoughts and actions with our desired state of well-being.

B. Visualization and Manifestation Techniques for Wellness

Visualization and manifestation techniques harness the power of our minds to create the reality we desire. By vividly imagining ourselves in a state of vibrant health and well-being, we activate the subconscious mind and stimulate positive change within ourselves. Visualization techniques involve creating mental images of our desired state, engaging our senses, and feeling the emotions associated with that state. Manifestation techniques, such as affirmations and scripting, help us solidify our intentions and reinforce positive beliefs about our well-being. By consistently practicing these techniques, we reprogram our minds and attract the experiences and circumstances that align with our vision of health and well-being.

C. Practicing Gratitude and Self-Love as Catalysts for Manifestation

Gratitude and self-love are powerful catalysts for *Manifesting Health and Well-Being*. Gratitude shifts our focus from what is lacking to what is abundant in our lives, creating a positive mindset and opening us up to receive more blessings. By regularly expressing gratitude for our bodies, minds, and spirits, we cultivate a deep appreciation for the gift of life and the inherent wisdom within us. Self-love involves nurturing ourselves with kindness, compassion, and acceptance. By honoring our needs, setting healthy boundaries, and practicing self-care, we create a strong foundation for well-being. When we approach our journey with gratitude and self-love, we magnetize positive experiences and attract the resources and opportunities that support our health and well-being.

Summary

Manifesting Health and Well-Being is a dynamic process that requires our active participation and engagement. By setting intentions for optimal health and well-being, we establish a clear direction for our journey. Utilizing visualization and manifestation techniques empowers us to create a vivid image of our desired state and attract positive experiences.

Practicing gratitude and self-love nourishes our hearts and minds, fostering a state of well-being from within. As we conclude this section, let us embrace these powerful techniques and practices as we move forward on our path of *Manifesting Health and Well-Being*, recognizing our inherent ability to create a life of vitality, balance, and wholeness.

Part 8: Overcoming Challenges and Building Resilience

On the journey to *Manifesting Health and Well-Being*, it is inevitable that we will encounter challenges and obstacles along the way. However, it is in these moments of adversity that our true strength and resilience are tested. In this section, we will explore strategies for overcoming setbacks, building resilience, and seeking support when needed. By adopting a proactive mindset, developing coping mechanisms, and reaching out for assistance, we can navigate challenges with grace and continue on the path to *Manifesting Health and Well-Being*.

A. Dealing with Setbacks and Obstacles on the Path to Well-Being

Setbacks and obstacles are a natural part of any transformative journey, including the pursuit of health and well-being. It is essential to recognize that setbacks do not define us, but rather provide opportunities for growth and learning. By reframing setbacks as temporary detours rather than permanent roadblocks, we can approach them with resilience and determination. Embracing a solution-oriented mindset, adapting our strategies when necessary, and staying committed to our overall well-being goals will enable us to navigate setbacks and continue moving forward on our path.

B. Building Resilience and Bouncing Back from Adversity

Resilience is the ability to bounce back from adversity and emerge stronger than before. Cultivating resilience is crucial for maintaining our well-being in the face of challenges. One way to build resilience is by developing healthy coping mechanisms that support our emotional and mental well-being. This may include practices such as journaling, mindfulness, meditation, or engaging in activities that bring us joy and relaxation. Additionally, fostering a positive mindset, cultivating self-compassion, and nurturing our support networks can contribute to our resilience and help us bounce back from adversity with greater ease.

C. Seeking Support and Professional Guidance When Needed
Recognizing when we need support and seeking assistance is a sign of strength, not weakness. When facing significant challenges on our journey to *Manifesting Health and Well-Being*, it can be immensely helpful to reach out to others for guidance and support. This support can come from trusted friends, family members, or professionals such as therapists, coaches, or healthcare practitioners. Their expertise and insights can provide valuable perspectives, tools, and strategies to overcome obstacles and navigate challenging times. By embracing the support available to us, we can accelerate our progress and maintain our well-being in a more sustainable and effective manner.

Summary
Overcoming challenges and building resilience are vital aspects of *Manifesting Health and Well-Being*. By recognizing setbacks as temporary and embracing a solution-oriented mindset, we can navigate obstacles with resilience and determination. Building resilience involves developing healthy coping mechanisms, fostering a positive mindset, and nurturing support networks. Seeking support from trusted individuals or professionals when needed is a strength that enhances our ability to overcome challenges. As we conclude this section, let us remember that setbacks do not define us; rather, they provide opportunities for growth and transformation. By building resilience and seeking support when needed, we can overcome obstacles on our path to *Manifesting Health and Well-Being*, ultimately leading to a life of vitality, balance, and fulfillment.

Part 9: Sustaining Long-Term Well-Being

Manifesting Health and Well-Being is not a destination but an ongoing journey that requires consistent effort and commitment. In this section, we will explore strategies for sustaining long-term well-being by cultivating a holistic lifestyle, embracing continuous learning and personal growth, and striking a balance between self-care and contributing to the well-being of others. By adopting these practices, we can create a sustainable foundation for our well-being and experience lasting vitality and fulfillment.

A. Cultivating a Holistic Lifestyle as an Ongoing Practice
Sustaining long-term well-being involves cultivating a holistic lifestyle that encompasses all aspects of our being—body, mind, and spirit. It requires nurturing our physical health through healthy eating, regular exercise, and adequate rest. Additionally, it involves nourishing our mental and emotional well-being through practices such as mindfulness, stress reduction techniques, and engaging in activities that bring us joy and fulfillment. By prioritizing self-care, setting boundaries, and integrating healthy habits into our daily routines, we can create a sustainable foundation for our overall well-being.

B. Continuous Learning and Personal Growth for Well-Being
Learning and personal growth are essential components of sustaining long-term well-being. Engaging in continuous learning allows us to expand our knowledge and understanding of ourselves and the world around us. It can involve reading books, attending workshops, taking courses, or seeking new experiences that challenge and inspire us. Personal growth involves introspection, self-reflection, and embracing opportunities for self-improvement. By remaining open to new ideas, perspectives, and experiences, we can continuously evolve and grow, enhancing our overall well-being.

C. Balancing Self-Care with Contributing to the Well-Being of Others
Sustaining long-term well-being requires finding a balance between self-care and contributing to the well-being of others. While it is crucial to prioritize our own self-care and ensure our needs are met, finding ways to support and contribute to the well-being of others can bring a deeper sense of purpose and fulfillment. This can involve acts of kindness, volunteering, or engaging in meaningful relationships and connections with others. By striking a balance between self-care and contributing to the well-being of others, we create a harmonious and fulfilling life that positively impacts both ourselves and those around us.

Summary

Sustaining long-term well-being is an ongoing practice that involves cultivating a holistic lifestyle, embracing continuous learning and personal growth, and balancing self-care with contributing to the well-being of others. By prioritizing our physical, mental, and emotional health, engaging in lifelong learning, and finding ways to support others, we create a sustainable foundation for *Manifesting Health and Well-Being*. Remember that this journey is not about perfection but about progress and consistent effort. As we conclude this section, let us embrace the idea that sustaining well-being is a lifelong commitment that brings lasting vitality, balance, and fulfillment to our lives.

Conclusion: Manifesting Health and Well-Being

In conclusion, *Manifesting Health and Well-Being* is a holistic endeavor that encompasses nurturing our body, mind, and spirit. By understanding the interconnectedness of these aspects and embracing practices that support our well-being, we can create a foundation for a vibrant and fulfilling life.

Throughout this chapter, we explored the definition and holistic nature of health and well-being, recognizing that they encompass much more than just physical health. We delved into the importance of self-care and self-awareness, acknowledging that taking care of ourselves is essential for our overall well-being.

We then explored different dimensions of well-being, starting with nurturing our physical health. By maintaining a balanced and nutritious diet, engaging in regular physical exercise, and ensuring adequate sleep and stress management, we can optimize our physical well-being.

Moving on to mental and emotional well-being, we discussed the significance of developing positive thought patterns and mindset, practicing mindfulness and stress reduction techniques, and building resilience to effectively manage emotions and challenges that come our way.

We also explored the realm of spiritual well-being, understanding that connecting with our spirituality, engaging in spiritual practices and rituals, and finding meaning and purpose in life contribute to our overall well-being.

Creating a healthy lifestyle involves incorporating healthy habits into our daily routines, building supportive relationships and social connections, and creating a nurturing and harmonious living environment. By surrounding ourselves with positivity and creating a conducive environment, we support our well-being.

Furthermore, we discussed holistic approaches to well-being, exploring alternative therapies and complementary modalities, integrating mind-body practices such as yoga and meditation, and embracing natural and sustainable living practices.

Manifesting Health and Well-Being requires setting intentions, utilizing visualization and manifestation techniques, and practicing gratitude and self-love as catalysts for manifestation. By aligning our thoughts, beliefs, and actions with our desired well-being, we can manifest a healthy and fulfilling life.

Finally, we explored overcoming challenges and building resilience, recognizing that setbacks and obstacles are a part of life's journey. By developing strategies to deal with setbacks, building resilience, and seeking support when needed, we can navigate through challenges and continue on our path to well-being.

Sustaining long-term well-being involves cultivating a holistic lifestyle as an ongoing practice, embracing continuous learning and personal growth, and balancing self-care with contributing to the well-being of others. By prioritizing our well-being, continuously evolving, and finding harmony in self-care and giving back, we can sustain our health and well-being throughout our lives.

Remember, *Manifesting Health and Well-Being* is not a destination but a lifelong journey. It requires commitment, self-awareness, and consistent effort. As you embark on this journey, may you nurture your body, mind, and spirit, and may you experience the profound joy and fulfillment that comes with *Manifesting Health and Well-Being*.

Chapter 10: Role of Patience and Trust: Surrendering to the Timing of the Universe

Welcome to the chapter on the "Role of Patience and Trust: Surrendering to the Timing of the Universe." In this chapter, we will delve into the profound significance of patience and trust in our personal growth and manifestation journey.

Patience and trust are not just mere virtues; they are powerful allies that can propel us forward on our path to success and fulfillment. In a world that often promotes instant gratification and quick results, understanding the value of patience and trust becomes even more crucial.

Patience allows us to navigate through the twists and turns of life, to stay committed to our goals, and to persevere in the face of challenges. It is the ability to remain calm and composed, even when things don't unfold as quickly as we desire. Trust, on the other hand, is the unwavering belief in the wisdom and timing of the universe. It is the surrender to the natural flow of life, knowing that everything happens for a reason and that the universe has our best interests at heart.

When it comes to personal growth and manifestation, patience and trust play a vital role. They help us release the need for control and allow us to embrace the journey, knowing that everything will unfold at the perfect time. By cultivating patience and trust, we open ourselves up to receiving the abundance and opportunities that the universe has in store for us.

In this chapter, we will explore the profound concepts of patience and trust and their impact on our lives. We will delve into the power of divine timing, understanding how the universe orchestrates events in our favor. We will discuss practical strategies for cultivating patience and trust, including developing self-awareness, practicing acceptance, and nurturing resilience.

Furthermore, we will explore the delicate balance between patience, trust, and action, discovering when to wait patiently and when to take inspired steps towards our desires. We will address common challenges such as impatience and doubt, providing insights and tools to overcome them.

Lastly, we will uncover the gifts that come from embracing patience and trust. We will recognize the blessings and growth that unfold when we surrender to the timing of the universe. Through this journey, we will learn to cultivate gratitude, appreciation, and a profound sense of peace as we align ourselves with the natural rhythm of life.

So, join us on this enlightening exploration of the *Role of Patience and Trust* in surrendering to the timing of the universe. Open your heart and mind to the transformative power that awaits as we embark on this journey together.

Part 1: Understanding Patience and Trust

In this section, we will delve into the fundamental aspects of patience and trust and their significance in our lives. As we explore the *Role of Patience and Trust* in surrendering to the timing of the universe, we will gain insights into their interconnectedness in the manifestation process.

A. Defining Patience and Its Significance in Our Lives

Patience is a virtue that allows us to endure difficulties and delays with calmness and composure. It is the ability to maintain a positive attitude and persevere, even in the face of challenges or when things don't unfold as quickly as we hope. Patience teaches us the value of waiting, of trusting the process, and of being present in the moment. It allows us to navigate life's uncertainties and setbacks while maintaining a sense of peace and inner balance. Patience plays a vital role in personal growth and manifestation as it cultivates resilience, self-discipline, and a deeper appreciation for the journey.

B. Exploring the Concept of Trust and Its Role in Surrendering to the Timing of the Universe

Trust is the unwavering belief in the wisdom and timing of the universe. It is the surrender to a higher power, knowing that everything happens for a reason and that there is a divine orchestration at play. Trust enables us to release the need for control and to embrace the flow of life. It allows us to let go of resistance and fear, opening ourselves up to infinite possibilities. Trusting in the timing of the universe means having faith that things will unfold at the perfect moment, aligning with our highest good and ultimate fulfillment.

C. Recognizing the Interconnectedness of Patience and Trust in the Manifestation Process

The *Role of Patience and Trust* in manifestation is intertwined. Patience is the foundation that supports our trust in the universe's timing. It enables us to remain steadfast in our desires and intentions, even when results aren't immediate. Patience helps us maintain a positive mindset and unwavering belief in the manifestation process. On the other hand, trust allows us to surrender control and release attachment to specific outcomes. It empowers us to embrace the present moment, knowing that the universe is working behind the scenes to align circumstances and opportunities for our highest good. Together, patience and trust create an environment of receptivity and alignment, facilitating the manifestation of our desires in divine timing.

Summary

Understanding the *Role of Patience and Trust* is crucial in our journey of surrendering to the timing of the universe. Patience teaches us resilience and the art of waiting, while trust instills a deep sense of faith in the universe's wisdom. These qualities work hand in hand to create a harmonious manifestation process, where we can gracefully align ourselves with the flow of life. In the following sections, we will explore practical strategies to cultivate and strengthen our patience and trust, empowering us to surrender and manifest with confidence and grace.

Part 2: The Power of Divine Timing

In this section, we will explore the profound concept of divine timing and its impact on our lives. By embracing the belief in divine timing, understanding the lessons it presents, and trusting in its inherent wisdom, we can align ourselves with the flow of the universe and experience a deeper sense of fulfillment and peace.

A. Embracing the Belief in Divine Timing and Its Influence on Our Lives

Divine timing refers to the idea that everything in the universe unfolds according to a higher plan and perfect timing. It is the understanding that there are unseen forces at work, orchestrating events and aligning circumstances for our highest good. Embracing the belief in divine timing allows us to let go of the need to control and micromanage every aspect of our lives. Instead, we can surrender to the unfolding of events, knowing that there is a greater wisdom guiding us. Divine timing reminds us that there are no accidents or coincidences, and that everything happens precisely when it needs to, even if we don't fully comprehend it in the present moment.

B. Understanding the Lessons and Growth Opportunities Presented by the Universe's Timing

The universe's timing is not arbitrary; it presents us with invaluable lessons and growth opportunities. Sometimes, delays or setbacks occur to teach us patience, resilience, or to redirect us towards a better path. Other times, seemingly fortuitous encounters or unexpected blessings come at just the right moment to propel us forward. By recognizing the lessons and growth opportunities in the timing of events, we can navigate our journey with greater awareness and gratitude. The *Role of Patience and Trust* becomes crucial here, as they allow us to embrace these lessons and growth experiences with grace and open-mindedness.

C. Trusting that Everything Unfolds in Perfect Timing for Our Highest Good

Trusting that everything unfolds in perfect timing is a powerful mindset to cultivate. It means having faith that the universe knows what is best for us, even when circumstances seem challenging or uncertain. Trust enables us to release the grip of fear and control, surrendering to a higher plan. When we trust in divine timing, we shift our perspective from impatience and doubt to a state of calm anticipation. We recognize that the universe has our best interests at heart and that every delay, detour, or synchronistic event serves a purpose in our personal growth and overall well-being. This trust empowers us to embrace the present moment fully and to navigate our journey with a sense of inner peace and contentment.

Summary
Understanding and embracing the power of divine timing allows us to release the burdens of impatience and control. By recognizing the influence of divine timing in our lives, we open ourselves up to profound growth, valuable lessons, and a deeper connection with the universe. As we trust that everything unfolds in perfect timing for our highest good, we can cultivate patience and unwavering faith. In the following sections, we will explore practical strategies to deepen our understanding of divine timing and strengthen our ability to surrender and trust, ultimately embracing the *Role of Patience and Trust* in manifesting a life aligned with the universe's timing.

Part 3: Cultivating Patience

In this section, we will explore the essential practice of cultivating patience and how it intertwines with the role of trust in surrendering to the timing of the universe. Patience is a virtue that allows us to navigate the ups and downs of life with grace, resilience, and a sense of inner calm. By developing self-awareness, practicing acceptance, and nurturing resilience, we can cultivate the invaluable quality of patience.

A. Developing Self-Awareness and Mindfulness to Cultivate Patience

Self-awareness is the foundation upon which patience is built. By becoming aware of our thoughts, emotions, and reactions, we can consciously choose how we respond to situations that test our patience. Mindfulness practices such as meditation, deep breathing, and present-moment awareness can help cultivate self-awareness and enhance our ability to stay grounded and composed in challenging moments. When we are aware of our triggers and tendencies, we can consciously choose patience as a response, allowing us to navigate difficulties with a greater sense of peace and understanding.

B. Practicing Acceptance and Letting Go of Control Over Outcomes

Patience often requires us to practice acceptance and surrender our need for control over outcomes. When we hold tightly to specific expectations and timelines, we create unnecessary stress and resistance. Instead, we can choose to trust in the timing of the universe and let go of our attachment to how things should unfold. By embracing the present moment and accepting what is, we release the struggle and find inner peace. Acceptance does not mean passivity; rather, it is an empowering choice to flow with the rhythm of life and trust in the unfolding process.

C. Nurturing Resilience and Perseverance in the Face of Delays or Challenges

Resilience and perseverance are key qualities that support patience. Building resilience involves developing the ability to bounce back from setbacks, learn from failures, and stay committed to our goals despite obstacles. By cultivating a growth mindset and viewing challenges as opportunities for growth, we can maintain a sense of optimism and determination. Patience requires us to stay focused on our long-term vision, even when faced with delays or challenges. It is through resilience and perseverance that we reinforce our trust in divine timing and maintain the strength to surrender and wait for the right moment.

Summary

Cultivating patience is a transformative practice that aligns us with the flow of life and the timing of the universe. By developing self-awareness, practicing acceptance, and nurturing resilience, we can cultivate patience as a guiding principle in our lives. The *Role of Patience and Trust* intertwines, creating a foundation of inner strength, resilience, and peace. As we continue our journey, the following sections will provide practical strategies and insights to further deepen our understanding and application of patience and trust in surrendering to the timing of the universe.

Part 4: Embracing Trust

In this section, we will explore the transformative power of trust and how it intertwines with the role of patience in surrendering to the timing of the universe. Trust is the foundation of faith and surrender, allowing us to let go of fear, embrace the unknown, and align with the flow of life. By building trust in ourselves, letting go of fear, and strengthening our connection with the universe, we can fully embrace trust and experience its profound impact on our lives.

A. Building Trust in Oneself and One's Abilities

Trust begins with developing a deep sense of self-belief and confidence. Building trust in ourselves involves acknowledging our strengths, honoring our experiences, and recognizing our capacity to overcome challenges. By celebrating our achievements, practicing self-compassion, and nurturing a positive self-image, we cultivate a strong foundation of trust in our own abilities. When we trust ourselves, we are better equipped to navigate uncertainty and make decisions aligned with our highest good.

B. Letting Go of Fear and Surrendering to the Flow of Life

Fear often inhibits our ability to trust. It holds us back from embracing new opportunities and surrendering to the natural flow of life. To fully embrace trust, we must confront and release our fears. By identifying the root causes of our fears and questioning their validity, we can diminish their power over us. Practicing courage and stepping outside our comfort zones allows us to experience the rewards that come with surrendering to the flow of life. Trusting that the universe has a plan for us brings a sense of freedom, allowing us to fully engage with the present moment and embrace the unfolding journey.

C. Strengthening Trust Through Faith, Intuition, and Alignment with the Universe

Trust is strengthened through our connection with something greater than ourselves. Developing faith, whether in a higher power, the universe, or the inherent goodness of life, provides a sense of support and guidance. Trusting in the wisdom of our intuition and aligning with the universe's energy helps us make choices that are in harmony with our true selves. By cultivating practices such as meditation, prayer, or connecting with nature, we deepen our trust and create space for divine guidance to unfold. The more we trust in the interconnectedness of all things, the more we can surrender to the timing of the universe and manifest our highest potential.

Summary
Embracing trust is a transformative journey that allows us to surrender to the timing of the universe and manifest our dreams and desires. By building trust in ourselves, letting go of fear, and strengthening our connection with the universe, we create a powerful foundation for embracing the *Role of Patience and Trust* in our lives. As we continue our exploration, the following sections will provide practical insights and strategies to further deepen our understanding and application of trust in surrendering to the timing of the universe.

Part 5: Finding Balance: Patience, Trust, and Action

In this section, we will delve into the art of finding balance between patience, trust, and taking inspired action. While patience and trust are essential in surrendering to the timing of the universe, they must be complemented by intentional action. It is through this delicate balance that we can actively co-create our reality and manifest our desires. By understanding when to wait and when to take steps forward, and by honoring the process while staying proactive, we can navigate the intricate dance of patience, trust, and action.

A. Balancing Patience and Trust with Taking Inspired Action

Patience and trust should not be mistaken for passivity. They work hand in hand with taking inspired action. While patience allows us to cultivate a state of calm and openness, trust empowers us to take the necessary steps towards our goals. Inspired action stems from a place of alignment with our deepest desires and intuition. By listening to our inner guidance, we can discern the appropriate actions to take and move forward with confidence and purpose. Balancing patience and trust with inspired action ensures that we are actively participating in the manifestation process.

B. Discerning When to Wait and When to Take Steps Towards Our Desires

Finding the right timing is a crucial aspect of manifesting our desires. Sometimes, patience requires us to wait for the optimal conditions to unfold. It involves trusting that the universe is orchestrating events in our favor, even if we cannot see it immediately. However, it is equally important to discern when it is time to take steps towards our desires. Through intuition and self-awareness, we can sense when the universe is calling us to act. By staying attuned to the signs and synchronicities around us, we can identify the opportune moments to move forward and seize the momentum of manifestation.

C. Honoring the Process While Staying Proactive in Co-Creating Our Reality

The journey of manifestation is a process that requires both patience and trust. It is essential to honor this process while remaining proactive in co-creating our reality. Patience allows us to embrace the present moment and find joy in the journey, knowing that every step is leading us closer to our desires. Trust reassures us that the universe is working in our favor, even when setbacks or challenges arise. It is through our proactive efforts, such as setting intentions, visualizing, and maintaining a positive mindset, that we align ourselves with the energy of manifestation. By combining patience, trust, and action, we actively participate in the unfolding of our dreams.

Summary

Finding balance among patience, trust, and action is a dynamic and transformative practice. By embracing patience and trust while taking inspired action, we navigate the intricate dance of co-creating our reality. Discerning when to wait and when to act allows us to align with the universe's timing, while honoring the process ensures that we stay proactive and engaged in our manifestation journey. As we continue to explore the *Role of Patience and Trust*, the following sections will provide practical insights and strategies to further cultivate this balance and manifest our desires.

Part 6: Overcoming Impatience and Doubt
In the manifestation journey, it is common to encounter moments of impatience and doubt. These emotions can hinder our progress and create obstacles on the path to manifesting our desires. However, by understanding how to identify and manage impatience and doubt, and by implementing strategies to counteract negativity, we can overcome these challenges and maintain a steadfast belief in the *Role of Patience and Trust*. In this section, we will explore practical approaches to cultivating a positive mindset, seeking support, and practicing self-compassion during times of impatience and doubt.

A. Identifying and Managing Impatience and Doubt in the Manifestation Journey
To effectively overcome impatience and doubt, it is crucial to first identify these emotions within ourselves. Impatience often arises when we feel that our desires are taking too long to materialize, while doubt creeps in when we question our abilities or the feasibility of our dreams. Recognizing these emotions allows us to take conscious steps towards managing them. By acknowledging and accepting our impatience and doubt, we can begin to shift our mindset and create space for patience and trust to flourish.

B. Cultivating Positive Mindset and Affirmations to Counteract Negativity
A positive mindset is a powerful tool in combating impatience and doubt. By consciously choosing positive thoughts and beliefs, we can counteract negativity and strengthen our trust in the manifestation process. Affirmations play a significant role in this practice. By repeating positive statements that align with our desires and aspirations, we rewire our subconscious mind and reinforce our belief in the inherent timing of the universe. Affirmations serve as constant reminders of our power to manifest and can help us stay focused and resilient during moments of impatience and doubt.

C. Seeking Support and Practicing Self-Compassion During Challenging Times

During challenging times, it is important to seek support from others and practice self-compassion. Surrounding ourselves with like-minded individuals who understand the manifestation journey can provide encouragement, guidance, and a sense of community. Sharing our struggles and successes with others not only validates our experiences but also reminds us that we are not alone in our journey. Additionally, practicing self-compassion is essential. It involves treating ourselves with kindness, understanding, and forgiveness. By practicing self-care, acknowledging our efforts, and celebrating our progress, we cultivate resilience and strengthen our belief in the *Role of Patience and Trust*.

Summary

Overcoming impatience and doubt is an integral part of the manifestation journey. By identifying and managing these emotions, cultivating a positive mindset through affirmations, seeking support, and practicing self-compassion, we can navigate through challenging times and reaffirm our belief in the *Role of Patience and Trust*. As we continue to explore the various facets of overcoming impatience and doubt, the following sections will provide further insights and practical strategies to empower us on our path towards manifestation success.

Part 7: The Gifts of Patience and Trust

Embracing patience and trust in the manifestation journey offers us profound gifts and opportunities for growth. By recognizing the blessings that come from cultivating these qualities, cultivating gratitude for the journey's timing, and harnessing the transformative power of surrendering to the timing of the universe, we can experience profound shifts in our lives. In this section, we will explore the gifts that patience and trust bestow upon us and how we can fully embrace and appreciate their role in our manifestation journey.

A. Recognizing the Blessings and Growth That Come from Embracing Patience and Trust

When we embody patience and trust, we open ourselves up to a world of blessings and growth. Patience allows us to savor each moment, appreciate the present, and experience personal transformation. It teaches us resilience, endurance, and the art of waiting for the perfect timing. Trust, on the other hand, enables us to release control and surrender to the natural flow of life. It invites miracles, synchronicities, and divine interventions into our journey. By embracing these qualities, we learn to let go of anxiety and resistance, paving the way for profound growth and personal development.

B. Cultivating Gratitude and Appreciation for the Journey and Its Timing

Gratitude is a powerful practice that amplifies the gifts of patience and trust. By cultivating gratitude for the journey and its timing, we shift our focus from what is lacking to what is present. We acknowledge the progress we have made, the lessons we have learned, and the experiences that have shaped us. Gratitude helps us recognize the beauty and significance of every step along the way, nurturing a sense of contentment and fulfillment. When we appreciate the journey and trust the timing, we align ourselves with the abundant flow of the universe, inviting even more blessings into our lives.

C. Harnessing the Transformative Power of Surrendering to the Timing of the Universe

Surrendering to the timing of the universe is a transformative act that allows us to release resistance and align with the greater intelligence at play. It requires us to relinquish the need for control and trust that everything is unfolding perfectly for our highest good. When we surrender, we let go of timelines, expectations, and limitations, and we open ourselves up to infinite possibilities. By surrendering, we invite the universe to work its magic, bringing forth the manifestation of our desires in the most perfect and divine timing. This surrender brings peace, clarity, and a profound sense of alignment with the flow of life.

Summary
Embracing patience and trust in our manifestation journey
bestows upon us extraordinary gifts. By recognizing the
blessings and growth that arise from these qualities,
cultivating gratitude and appreciation for the journey and its
timing, and harnessing the transformative power of
surrender, we open ourselves to a world of possibilities and
align ourselves with the abundant flow of the universe. As we
continue to explore the profound gifts that patience and trust
offer, the subsequent sections will provide further insights
and practical strategies to help us fully embrace and
appreciate their role in manifesting our dreams.

Conclusion: Role of Patience and Trust

In conclusion, the *Role of Patience and Trust* in our journey
of manifesting our desires is undeniably significant. By
understanding the essence of patience and its significance in
our lives, exploring the concept of trust and its role in
surrendering to the timing of the universe, and recognizing
the interconnectedness of patience and trust in the
manifestation process, we can embark on a transformative
path towards realizing our dreams.

Patience teaches us the art of waiting, resilience in the face of
challenges, and the ability to trust in the unfolding of divine
timing. It allows us to embrace each moment, savor the
journey, and grow personally and spiritually. Trust, on the
other hand, invites us to release control, surrender to the flow
of life, and have faith in the greater plan. It opens the doors to
synchronicities, miracles, and aligning with the abundant
possibilities that the universe holds.

Cultivating patience requires self-awareness, mindfulness,
acceptance, and nurturing resilience in the face of delays or
challenges. It empowers us to stay proactive in co-creating
our reality while honoring the natural timing of the universe.
Similarly, embracing trust involves building trust in ourselves
and our abilities, letting go of fear, and strengthening our
faith, intuition, and alignment with the universe.

Finding balance becomes crucial as we navigate the
intersection of patience, trust, and action. Balancing inspired

action with waiting, discerning when to take steps towards our desires, and honoring the process allows us to actively participate in co-creating our reality while surrendering to the divine timing of the universe.

Throughout the journey, it's natural to encounter impatience and doubt. However, by identifying and managing these challenges, cultivating a positive mindset, practicing affirmations, seeking support, and showing self-compassion, we can overcome these obstacles and continue on our path with renewed determination and resilience.

Ultimately, the gifts of patience and trust are abundant. Recognizing the blessings and growth that come from embracing these qualities, cultivating gratitude for the journey and its timing, and harnessing the transformative power of surrendering to the timing of the universe, we align ourselves with the abundant flow of life, inviting miracles and profound shifts into our lives.

As we continue to nurture patience and trust in our lives, we embark on a journey of self-discovery, personal growth, and manifestation. May these qualities guide us towards our dreams, and may we find solace in surrendering to the timing of the universe, knowing that everything unfolds in perfect alignment with our highest good. Embrace patience, trust the process, and allow the universe to work its magic in manifesting your desires.

Discover the transformative power of patience and trust in surrendering to the divine timing of the universe, as you embark on a journey of self-discovery, personal growth, and manifestation.

Epilogue

As we come to the end of *The Manifestation Blueprint: Cracking the Code to Abundance*, I invite you to take a moment to reflect on the transformative journey we have embarked upon together. Throughout this book, we have explored the profound principles and practices that empower you to manifest the life of your dreams and unlock the abundant possibilities that await you.

We began by uncovering *The Power of Manifestation: Unleashing Your Inner Potential*. You discovered that within you lies an extraordinary power, capable of shaping your reality and bringing your desires to life. You learned to tap into this power and harness it to manifest the life you truly deserve.

In *Understanding the Law of Attraction: Creating Your Reality*, you delved into the universal principles that govern manifestation. You gained a deep understanding of how your thoughts and emotions shape the world around you and learned to use the Law of Attraction to your advantage.

The *Art of Visualization: Painting Your Dreams into Existence* became your creative tool for manifesting. You learned to vividly imagine your desired outcomes, infusing them with emotion and detail, and aligning your actions with the visions you hold in your mind's eye.

Harnessing the Energy of Manifestation: Aligning Your Thoughts and Emotions revealed the profound connection between your thoughts and emotions and their influence on the manifestation process. By aligning your inner world with your desires, you harnessed the energetic power needed to attract and manifest your dreams.

Setting Clear Intentions: Navigating Your Path to Success became your compass on this journey. You discovered the importance of defining your goals with clarity and purpose, and staying focused on your intentions as you navigated the path to success.

Overcoming Limiting Beliefs: Rewriting Your Subconscious Mind empowered you to identify and release the self-sabotaging beliefs that have held you back. Through effective techniques, you reprogrammed your subconscious mind with empowering beliefs that support your manifestation journey.

Cultivating Gratitude and Abundance: Opening the Floodgates of Manifestation taught you the transformative practice of gratitude. By embracing a mindset of abundance and cultivating gratitude for what you have and what is yet to come, you opened the floodgates for more abundance to flow into your life.

Creating Wealth and Prosperity: Abundance as Your Birthright expanded your understanding of wealth and prosperity. You explored strategies to attract financial abundance, create multiple streams of income, and manifest a life of prosperity in all areas.

Manifesting Health and Well-Being: Nurturing Your Body, Mind, and Spirit revealed the importance of holistic well-being in the manifestation journey. By nurturing your physical, mental, and spiritual health, you created a solid foundation for manifesting a life of vitality and well-being.

Finally, we explored the *Role of Patience and Trust*: Surrendering to the Timing of the Universe. You recognized that manifestation is a process that unfolds in divine timing. By cultivating patience and trust, you learned to surrender to the timing of the universe, overcoming impatience and doubt, and allowing your desires to manifest in their perfect timing.

As we conclude this remarkable journey together, remember that the power to manifest your dreams lies within you. The tools, insights, and practices shared in *The Manifestation Blueprint* have equipped you with the knowledge and understanding to create a life of abundance. Trust in yourself and the universe and continue to apply these principles in your daily life.

Now is the time to embrace your innate potential and step into a reality where abundance is your natural state. The world is ready to receive your manifestations, and the universe is conspiring to support your desires. With each intentional thought, aligned action, and unwavering trust, you are actively co-creating the abundant life you deserve.

I am grateful to have been your guide on this transformative journey, and I invite you to carry the wisdom and practices you have gained with you as you continue to manifest your dreams. Remember, the power to create your reality resides within you. Embrace it, trust in it, and watch as the manifestation of your desires unfolds before your eyes.

Congratulations on embarking on this extraordinary path to abundance. Your future is filled with limitless possibilities, and I have no doubt that you will continue to manifest a life beyond your wildest dreams. May you always live in alignment with your true desires and experience the abundant blessings that are your birthright.

Wishing you a life of abundance, joy, and fulfillment as you continue to crack the code to your own unique manifestation blueprint.

Printed in Great Britain
by Amazon